FAREWELL TO MAY'S BOUNTY

HAMPSHIRE COUNTY CRICKET

at

Basingstoke

1906-2000

By

Kevin Smallbone

ACKNOWLEDGEMENTS

Firstly I would like to express my gratitude to Mark Nicholas for his entertaining and heartfelt foreword. I am also indebted to all those who provided photographs, particularly to Dave Allen and Vic Isaacs of Hampshire County Cricket Club, Bill Browne the Editor in Chief of *Gazette Newspapers,* Pam Ludgate of Basingstoke and North Hants Cricket Club (B&NHCC), my brother Bernie Smallbone, and all other copyright holders. Thanks also to Steve Partridge for reading the proofs and for his help and advice generally, to Ernie Major of the Willis Museum, and to Basingstoke's historian Arthur Attwood MBE.

ISBN 0-9537880-1-6

The front cover photograph of Shane Warne comes courtesy of *Gazette Newspapers* and the cigarette cards are from a series by Godfrey Phillips Ltd. Rear cover – thanks to B&NHCC for the photograph of the Hampshire team at May's Bounty in 1906 and to the *Gazette Newspapers* for the photograph of Robin Smith. The Hampshire v. Durham match scene is by Bernie Smallbone, and cigarette cards by kind permission of Imperial Tobacco Ltd, England.

BY THE SAME AUTHOR

The Story of the Basingstoke Derby Match – Basingstoke Town v. Thornycroft Athletic 1900-1972.
ISBN 0-9537880-0-8
A paperback which is available by post by sending a cheque for £7.00 (including P&P) payable to St Michael's Hospice (North Hampshire) at Basil de Ferranti House, Aldermaston Road, Basingstoke RG24 7NB.

CONTENTS

FOREWORD by Mark Nicholas

Having to say "Farewell to May's Bounty" seems to me so sad. Not that the cricket ground is going, just that Hampshire can no longer find a place for it in this commercially driven modern environment for sport.

I loved playing at this oh, so friendly place which welcomed players with unconditional warmth. A good pitch, though never particularly fast, offered something for everyone but the speed of the outfield and the size of the boundaries inclined the advantage to batsmen. I even rather liked the dressing rooms which were tiny and quirky, but home.

My first home match for Hampshire was at May's Bounty in 1978 and Zaheer Abbas, that sublime stroke-maker from Pakistan, amazed me with the ease and accuracy of his placement either side of us helpless fielders. Mike Procter, a boyhood hero, was playing too and hit straight sixes and bowled both fast and slow. What a cricketer!

My most vivid memory of the match, however, is of standing at first slip to Andy Roberts who rocked down the hill and bowled near the speed of light. By fluke I caught an edge at bootlace height and the team said they had found a new slipper. I said "you're joking, I haven't seen one that he's bowled yet".

In 1980, eleven runs short of a first championship hundred, I was run out by a deflection at the non-strikers end against Glamorgan. It all but broke my heart which was quickly mended by the incomparable reception I received from the most supportive, sympathetic audience who watched us play.

A year later Jeff Thomson, steaming down the hill for Middlesex, hit me in t he ...er .. well, you-know-whats. And I thought Roberts was quick. Writhing around the crease I implored the doctor to take away the pain but leave the swelling. Mike Brearley, Middlesex's captain, was unconvinced by the severity of the damage or the theatricals which followed and said "it's perfectly apparent your mother was an actress." I was stretchered off.

Then came the Marshall years and the chance to have someone tearing down the hill on our behalf. And how. In one game Marshall ripped through Surrey twice in a day – yes Surrey, lovely job – and then we played an exhibition match on the Saturday in front of a good crowd and beat them again. Just as lovely.

There are so many memories of this beautiful, cosy ground to play cricket. Sachin Tendulkar batted there for Yorkshire but didn't get many. Robin Smith decimated Derbyshire in a mammoth and successful run chase when we were serious championship contenders in 1985. Ten years later Cardigan Connor decimated Leicestershire with his intelligent and always gutsy seam and swing. Actually, I have just remembered playing at Basingstoke for the second XI in 1977 when Leicestershire's new-ball attack was Alan Ward and Ken Shuttleworth - it was, honest. I don't think we got many.

Hampshire won a lot at May's Bounty which helps with the romance of course but when we lost I used to arrive in orbit with rage. My worst memory is of a Sunday match in 1993 when the Kent openers, Trevor Ward and Mathew Fleming, took full advantage of the then seemingly ridiculous new restrictions on field placing in the first fifteen overs. Only two fielders were allowed outside a thirty yard ring and on a perfect pitch Malcolm was for once, and one of the only times, smashed to all parts.

By heaven, they hit him everywhere and being past his best, and way past his fastest, he had nothing left with which to respond. It hurt him badly and afterwards, both of us fuelled by brandy, he told me he was going to retire. Through the alcohol and the emotion I had to agree.

Anyway, these ramblings could go on forever. Thank you May's Bounty, and the host of folk who worked feverishly on our behalf, for your friendship and hospitality. It was always a hard bar to leave of an evening, it is an even harder cricket ground to bid farewell.

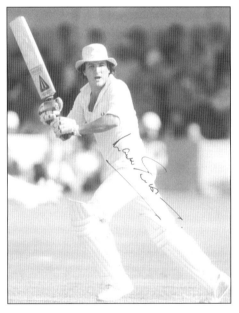

Mark Nicholas in action
[Photo: Mark Leech]

PREFACE

Cricket-mad youngsters who, like me, grew up in Basingstoke in the 1950s and early 1960s were deprived of the opportunity to watch their Hampshire idols appearing at May's Bounty. Not that we were aware of such deprivation since we did not realise that in the past Hampshire immortals such as Phil Mead and, amongst opposing teams, the likes of the legendary bodyline bowlers Larwood and Voce had once graced the same turf as our more familiar Basingstoke heroes such as Guy Jewell, Maurice Smith and David Gifford. This was the very same turf, too, on which we ourselves were later thrilled to play the occasional Queen Mary's School match and in the evening limited overs knockout competition, later called the Guy Jewell Cup.

Without exposure on television, county cricket was a considerable leap in the imagination for us and, in practical terms, was a 9s.6d. train ride away at Southampton. It was to be in 1958 that I was to see my first county match at Southampton and was to witness for the first time the well-oiled arm of Derek Shackleton secure its usual five-wicket haul.

Always a disappointing sight for spectators –
the return of ROY MARSHALL to the pavilion

Our real favourite, however, was inevitably to be Roy Marshall whose cavalier strokeplay made him the fastest-scoring and most exciting batsman in English county cricket at that time, only rivalled perhaps by Ted Dexter for Sussex and Colin Milburn for Northamptonshire. Roy Marshall was not a player to be adopted by the faint-hearted, however, since he always lived on the edge - and we lived every ball with him. On a number of occasions we arrived a few minutes after the start of play - especially at Bournemouth where the train from Basingstoke did not quite tie in time-wise - to find that he was already back in the pavilion and that the Hampshire start had to be repaired by Jimmy Gray and Henry Horton, players whose more prosaic qualities had less appeal for impatient youth but were to become more appreciated by us over the years. If Marshall fell in the first over it was quite possible that he would have been caught off a top edge at third man, perhaps second ball for six!

We always knew the Basingstoke ground by its original name - the 'Folly'. But it had been re-named May's Bounty in 1881 as a tribute to Lt. Col. John May who had bought the ground the year before in order to preserve it for sporting activities. Unbeknown to us, Hampshire county cricket matches had in fact been played there since 1906, although only intermittently. There were two games before the First World War and a run of Championship matches in the 1930s, and then a long wait, punctuated only by a visit by the Oxford University team in 1951, before the county team appeared again at the ground - in 1966, ironically Roy Marshall's first year as captain. Since then we Basingstoke-based supporters have enjoyed yearly visits by Hampshire for a Championship fixture and also since 1969 for Sunday League games as well. That we were to see many of the great players in world cricket at the Folly would have seemed inconceivable to us as youngsters.

The loss of that annual opportunity - with all matches to be centred on the new ground at Southampton - is sad indeed. And this time the deprivation will be keenly felt. The north of the county has always been the 'poor relation' in terms of the first-class game - but this finally banishes it from the family altogether and denies May's Bounty the opportunity in 2006 to celebrate the centenary of the first county cricket match at the ground. Both captain Robin Smith and vice-captain, the Basingstoke-based Shaun Udal, have expressed their regret but naturally have to back the club's decision. Former captain Mark Nicholas, who so often made runs at May's Bounty, has been more openly critical. Smith, who has scored more runs at the ground in first-class cricket than any other batsman, said he had always enjoyed playing there. And now, as captain, he felt that their knowledge of the May's Bounty wicket would give them an advantage over visitors Durham. Shaun Udal said that he was sad and disappointed at having to lose this venue because it always provided a good atmosphere and made the match a real occasion.

The decision was made on financial grounds in order to make maximum returns on the investment in the new ground - though it is worth noting that the fixture is always very well supported and that the County Club have used the May's Bounty ground free of charge. Inevitably, money is the determining factor in the modern first-class game but when it is the *only* consideration then we risk losing the very essence of the great game of cricket. The eventual outcome could be a standard packaged product cut off from its own roots, the rich pattern of the game giving way to a dull uniformity. Similar debates have, however, attended the game of cricket for a century or more as it has sought to balance aesthetic and commercial considerations and to adapt to changing times to ensure its survival. That very survival – of a spectator sport played at a time when most of its potential customers are not available to watch it - is a remarkable achievement in itself.

This book gives an account of the record of Hampshire CCC at May's Bounty and tries to capture something of the flavour of occasions now apparently consigned to history – first-class cricket matches played in delightful surroundings and in a setting which still conjures up something of the feeling of how cricket may have been in the so-called 'Golden Age'.

The May's Bounty crowd relaxes during an interval in play in the final County match. Fairfields School, which was attended by a young John Arlott, is in the background.

A view from the members' enclosure – Hampshire v. Durham in progress

THE YEAR 2000

CHAPTER ONE

The Last County Match at May's Bounty?

It has been said that May's Bounty is the most beautiful place in Basingstoke – not an extravagant claim these days it must be said. And its very name has intrigued many visitors – once described as "the most gorgeous name ever to adorn a cricket ground" (*Guide to County Cricket,* 1993 ed. R. Steen). It is worth reflecting that but for John May's intervention it would now simply be yet another housing estate, the very fate which sadly now awaits the Northlands Road ground in Southampton with its fine Victorian pavilion.

The Bounty Inn, Basingstoke with the AA sign in place for the final county match. It was previously named the Cattle Market Inn, reflecting the former usage of Fairfields as the area for cattle and sheep fairs *[photo: Bernie Smallbone]*

The May's Bounty pitch which was to come under the microscope

Players, spectators, and journalists alike are almost always complimentary about May's Bounty, particularly the friendly and intimate atmosphere of the ground. Robin Smith has always said how much he enjoys playing there and his brother Chris named the ground in his top ten favourite grounds around the world. The only discordant voices, on occasion, have been the odd pitch inspector or losing captain complaining about the standard of the wicket. It *is* difficult to maintain standards on what is essentially a club wicket but May's Bounty is by no means untypical of wickets all over the country in offering something to the bowlers. This topic was to be aired once more in this match but this time it was to be the dryness of the pitch which was to be the subject of debate.

The build-up to the final county match programmed for May's Bounty in June 2000 was full of controversy as the campaign to have the ground re-instated as a venue for Hampshire cricket gathered pace but made no headway. But on the day the crowd was merely intent on enjoying this last match. There were no signs of protest nor were campaigners out in force with requests for petitions to be signed.

Despite the overcast weather on the first morning – low cloud was to remain throughout the match – the ground looked an absolute picture with an excellent crowd for a weekday match not in the main holiday season. No one could fail to be impressed by May's Bounty when it has been prepared for the big occasion and is bedecked with marquees nestling amongst the trees which line the boundary's edge. Only the advertising hoardings – and perhaps the absence of the odd Harlequin cap or cravat – could persuade us that this was not an Edwardian scene. We were greeted with the unusual sight of players practising in a net put up at the edge of the square very adjacent to the strip to be used for the match. With spectators able to watch this so close-up it served to emphasise one of the attractive features of the ground – its intimacy and informality.

There was little apparent excitement, but there was a sense of occasion, a feeling that this was a historic moment. Constant exposure on television breeds familiarity even for the most famous celebrities nowadays, but for those of us born and bred in Basingstoke it took a little comprehending that here, in this homely little ground, was Shane Warne - looking every inch the year 2000 superstar, bleached hair and all, one of Wisden's five Cricketers of the Century - having a net, signing autographs and preparing to play for Hampshire.

SHANE WARNE returns to the pavilion to prepare for the Durham innings

On the fixture list at the start of the season the clash with Durham would not have appeared to be the most attractive fixture for the last county match at Basingstoke. But now it was a vital bottom of the table contest. In the previous season Hampshire had surprised a lot of commentators in achieving First Division status in the first year of the 2-division PPP County Championship in 2000. Then in the close season they had pulled off the tremendous coup of acquiring none other than Shane Warne as their overseas player, together with re-signing the England left-arm pace bowler Alan Mullally. This so transformed people's perceptions of

Hampshire's prospects that at the beginning of the new season they were being mentioned in some quarters as potential champions. This, together with the great excitement over the new ground at West End to be finally ready in 2001, created a feeling of great expectation not experienced since the heady days of Richards and Greenidge.

Then cold reality took a hand to the extent that Hampshire were soon propping up the First Division and still remained without a Championship win as they approached the clash with Durham, one place above them. The main failing was the inabiltiy to build totals, particularly in the first innings, which were sufficient to give the bowlers a chance. Shane Warne took time to settle and was not helped by the wet wickets, while Alan Mullally had injury problems. For those who believe that history repeats itself this was a worrying start since a century ago Hampshire suffered a similar run and actually ended the season of 1900 without a single win from 22 games! They also went on to receive the wooden spoon in successive years in 1902/3/4 and 5.

Day One
However, Hampshire's record at May's Bounty over the years is a good one, particularly recently with a run of four consecutive Championship wins only having been broken by Yorkshire's visit in 1999. So the county's supporters remained optimistic, particularly when Hampshire – including both spinners Warne and Udal in their line-up - won the toss and elected to bat first on a dry-looking wicket which seemed to promise the prospect of turn later in the match.

But the challenge now was to build a good first innings score on what looked like a bowlers' day. There was heavy cloud cover and Durham boasted a strong pace attack. Steve Harmison had been released for the game from the England squad for the Test Match against the West Indies, and Simon Brown, himself with an England cap to his credit, formed the opening attack with an array of supporting medium pacers headed by Melvyn Betts, an England 'A' player.

Hampshire, desperate for more solidity at the top of the order, had turned to 20 year-old Andrew Sexton and he was making his fist-class debut after some good scores in Minor Counties cricket with Dorset. Right from the first ball, placed wide of gully for four by Giles White, things went well for the home county. Sexton, a left-hander, settled in calmly and played back a maiden over from the pacey Harmison bowling up the hill. He opened his account in the fourth over with a glide off his legs and went on to make a good impression, playing straight and making some pleasant shots particularly off his legs. Together the new pairing put on 62, Hampshire's highest opening partnership of the season, before White was caught at second slip in Harmison's second spell, generating good pace and bounce down the hill from the Castle Field end, and Sexton fell lbw to Betts for 36 just before lunch at 105-2.

Welcome to first-class cricket – SEXTON ducks a delivery from Harmison
[photo: courtesy of Gazette Newspapers]

WILL KENDALL cuts in his innings of 42 *[photo: courtesy of Gazette Newspapers]*

Vic Isaacs, the Hampshire scorer and PA announcer, was experiencing problems, not having had a telephone line installed to keep him informed of scores from other grounds around the country and to allow him in turn to feed the match scores to Teletext. The problem was to remain on the second day too, and he was only able to keep the crowd up to date with details of the all-too-regular fall of England wickets in the Test Match with the help of a nearby spectator's radio.

In the afternoon Robin Smith snicked his second ball for four, then unleashed a ferocious trademark square cut for another, and we wondered whether it was to be his day - as it had been so often at May's Bounty. Alas it was not to be this time but, well partnered by Will Kendall, he still played an entertaining knock of 43 before unluckily gloving to the wicket-keeper down the leg side. 171-2 became 176-4 with their departures and this is the point at which the Hampshire innings, true to the season's form, would have collapsed.

But Derek Kenway and Adrian Aymes purposefully put together an unbroken stand of 79 in 30 overs to steady the ship and put Hampshire in a promising position at 255-4 when bad light intervened to close the day 18 overs short. Only Kendall had lost his wicket to a ball that misbehaved but there were already signs on this first day that the wicket was starting to dust.

A puff of dust on the first day – Betts to Smith : *photo Bernie Smallbone]*

Close of play on the first day. The May's Bounty scoreboard was erected in 1949. [photo: Bernie Smallbone]

Day Two

The second day proved just as overcast and humid as the first and in helpful conditions Simon Brown produced an excellent spell of swing bowling, left-arm over from the Castle Field end, and he had both overnight batsman lbw for the addition of only 21 runs in the first hour. But the top six in Hampshire the order had all contributed significantly.

A fine spell of bowling from Simon Brown – Mascarenhus facing [photo Bernie Smallbone]

So the scene was set for Shane Warne's entry to the fray – but to a surprisingly muted welcome from the Basingstoke public. He soon collected his fifth championship duck of the season, Brown's third victim in ten balls, and departed in virtual silence save for his own muttering to the incoming Udal that "it's swinging out there". But Basingstoke was to warm considerably to Warne's contributions over the next few days.

ALAN MULLALLY's languid return to the pavilion

There was much playing and missing at Betts, too, Harmison having departed with sore shins. It was proving very difficult to penetrate the field, with Shaun Udal and Dimitri Mascarenhas trying to consolidate in indifferent light (one light was glowing on the scoreboard even before lunch). But they managed a flurry of fours to raise their stand to a precious 41 runs before Mascarenhus nicked the last ball of the morning to wicket-keeper Martin Speight at 315-8.

In the first over after lunch Udal struck two good fours and also played and missed twice, while Alan Mullally did not linger. Brown then claimed his fourth wicket as Udal's useful knock ended, nicking one down the leg side, and Hampshire were all out for 340.

Cloud cover remained as the Durham innings began, facing good tight opening overs from Mullally down the hill and from the lively Simon Francis. John Lewis soon popped one up off Mullally to be caught by White at short leg before a run had been scored. Then Masceranhus, relieving an unlucky Francis at the town end, began a very good spell, swinging the ball as well as getting some awkward lift. He trapped the Australian Katich lbw second ball and then had both Collingwood and the very promising seventeen year-old Nick Penn snapped up in the slips at 22-4.

Shane Warne was thrown the ball after 13 overs and was not to relinquish it again. He began with a testing maiden from the town end. He soon started to extract some sharp turn from a dusty track, while Mullally was swinging the ball in the heavy atmosphere. Although captain Nick Speak and wicket-keeper Martin Speight offered some resistance in the middle of the innings, once they fell the floodgates were open and Warne bamboozled the lower order batsmen to dismiss Durham for just 83.

May's Bounty had witnessed a spell of spin bowling of the very highest class. Durham had faced international quality bowling in helpful conditions, but it seemed unlikely that the wicket had deteriorated sufficiently to justify such a capitulation. Following on, Durham as early as the third over were facing the two Hampshire spinners in tandem. Udal soon trapped young Penn lbw, while Warne had as many as eight fielders round the bat as Durham finished the day at 12-1.

Seventeen wickets had fallen in the day but overnight the national press felt that no blame should attach to the May's Bounty pitch. We subsequently learned that

SHANE WARNE begins his classic spell at May's Bounty [photo courtesy of Gazette Newspapers]

the umpires, Tony Clarkson and former Hampshire all-rounder Trevor Jesty, contacted the ECB to submit a "precautionary" report. This was to become a familiar occurrence at grounds all round the country during the season.

Day Three
Despite a more promising weather forecast the third day saw heavy cloud cover once more, helpful conditions for swing bowling which were again exploited by Mullally as he had Lewis snapped up at slip in the third over and then nightwatchman Betts lbw at 31-3. But it was when the spinners were in tandem again, off and leg spin perfectly paired, that one felt that Durham were facing the crunch. Udal removed Collingwood via a diving catch by White at short leg to make it 59-4. We also had the unique event at Basingstoke of Aussie bowling to Aussie, Warne to Katich. Warne first had Speak caught at the wicket and then the left-handed Katich, who had played well for a top score of 26, caught at slip from a googly. With Harmison unable to bat the remaining tail offered little resistance on a surface offering turn and bounce to the world's premier spin bowler, and Durham subsided tamely to a final score of 93 and to defeat by an innings and 164 runs just before lunch on the third day of four. Eight wickets had fallen in the morning. Shane Warne had finished with match figures of 8 for 56 and had received good support from Mullally in both innings and from Mascarenhus in the first and Udal in the second.

14

WARNE spills a slip catch off fellow spinner SHAUN UDAL *[photo: courtesy of Gazette Newspapers]*

ADRIAN AYMES in action *[photo: courtesy of Gazette Newspapers]*

Pitch Controversy

So May's Bounty had come up trumps again for Hampshire whose first taste of Championship success this was in 2000. It was the result – but not the match – that the Basingstoke faithful had wanted to see. It had brought Hampshire a precious 18 points. But not without controversy. The Durham coach, Norman Gifford, said afterwards that the pitch was so dry that it was not fit for first-class cricket. He felt that winning the toss had conferred a crucial advantage because even on the first day one or two balls had "gone through the top". But the ECB representatives, Tony Brown and Mike Denness, only marked the pitch "below average" which meant that Hampshire were not penalised. Most commentators concluded that while conditions were not easy the main factor in Durham's defeat had been their very limp response to the adverse conditions that confronted them. It did not help that they went into the match with only Phillips' occasional off-breaks providing an alternative to swing and seam.

A job well done – Hampshire players leave the field. Shaun Udal in the foreground, while Dimitri Mascarenhas obliges a young autograph-hunter

THE SCORECARD
County Championship
Hampshire v. Durham at May's Bounty, 14, 15, and 16 June 2000

HAMPSHIRE First Innings

G White c Collingwood b Harmison	29
A Sexton lbw b Betts	36
W Kendall c Phillips b Collingwood	42
R Smith c Speight b Collingwood	43
D Kenway lbw b Brown	47
A Aymes lbw b Brown	40
D Mascarenhas c Speight b Wood	27
S Warne c Speight b Brown	0
S Udal c Speight b Brown	35
A Mullally lbw b Betts	0
S Francis not out	5
Extras	36
Total (126.1 overs)	340

Bowling:
Brown 22.1-3-62-4
Harmison 19-6-33-1
Wood 24-4-94-1
Phillips 13-4-23-0
Collingwood 15-5-34-2
Katich 3-1-2-0

DURHAM First Innings		**Second Innings**	
J Lewis c White b Mullally	0	c Kendall b Mullally	3
N Peng c Kendall b Mascarenhas	9	lbw b Udal	0
S Katich lbw b Mascarenhas	2	c Kendall b Warne	26
P Collingwood c Warne b Mascarenhas	6	c White b Udal	13
N Speak c Sexton b Warne	22	c Aymes b Warne	6
M Speight c Kendall b Mullally	12	b Warne	17
N Phillips lbw b Mullally	1	c Kendall b Warne	2
J Wood c Aymes b Warne	11	c Mascarenhas b Udal	1
M Betts b Warne	12	lbw b Mullally	23
S Brown c Mascarenhas b Warne	1	not out	2
S Harmison not out	0	absent	
Extras	7		0
Total (49.4 overs)	83	Total (42.3 overs)	93

Bowling:

Mullally	17-9-18-3	7-3-12-2	
Francis	4--2-6-0	4-2-10-0	
Mascarenhas	8-3-17-3	6-1-14-0	
Warne	18.4 -7-34-4	11-2-22-4	
Udal	2-1-3-0	14.3-2-35-3	

Hampshire won by an innings and 164 runs

The modern-day Pavilion

The Sunday League Match

Success breeds success and sure enough Hampshire, transformed into Hampshire Hawks, went on to beat Durham Dynamos by 18 runs in their limited overs match two days later, their first win of the season in that competition too - the National Cricket League. Hampshire set a target of 222, with Smith providing the impetus with 43 in 56 balls, and John Stephenson the backbone, batting through the innings for 83 not out. Durham looked well set for victory at 95 for no wicket in 20 overs, but once Shane Warne had broken the opening partnership and the overseas player Simon Katich was quickly run out, they lost their way. They were eventually all out for 204, mainly due to a superb second spell from Mullally (4-40) which was in sharp contrast to his first three overs which had been laced with frequent leg-side wides.

Ironically this Sunday match brought a gloriously sunny day – so hot that the scoreboard almost gave up in the heat - and the Basingstoke public turned out in force for Hampshire's last appearance. It was wonderful to see May's Bounty so packed for such an occasion. As the match moved to its climax, above the good-humoured and excited hubbub which attended the closing overs, could be detected a lone tenor voice – a very melodic voice - which seemed to offer a final poignant lament to the loss of this lovely ground to the first-class game, one of the most attractive venues in the country.

Basingstoke's benefactor Lt. Col. John May would doubtless have had less affinity for the paraphernalia of the one-day arena – with its coloured clothing, white ball, red stumps and black sight screens – but he could still have related to the more traditional format of Championship cricket. As the crowd dispersed from this final match one could not help but think back to his triumph in 1906 when he had managed to get the Hampshire club to come to Basingstoke to play a Championship game at May's Bounty for the first time.

Scenes from the Sunday League match v. Durham at May's Bounty

[photos: Bernie Smallbone]

A packed May's Bounty basking in the sunshine

The scoreboard which almost gave up in the heat

More Sunday League Scenes

Between innings – time to stretch the legs and to seek refreshment

A match-winning spell from Alan Mullally

THE GOLDEN AGE

CHAPTER TWO

…And The First:

"Spirit of this kind makes cricket worth playing"

The Folly

It must have brought considerable satisfaction to Lt. Col. John May as President of Basingstoke and North Hants Cricket Club that by 1906 he had presided over the transformation of what was no more than a meadow into the club's permanent home and ultimately into an enclosure fit to stage first-class cricket. It was some achievement that Hampshire were to stage a County Championship match in Basingstoke for the first time, hitherto a privilege exclusive to grounds in the south of the county, except for one visit by the county team to Aldershot the previous season.

John May was a key personality in the history and development of Basingstoke, a partner in the May's Brewery, Mayor on six separate occasions and a benefactor of the town in many ways. In sport, as well as playing a pivotal role in the early development of cricket, he also did much to stimulate football, presenting the May Challenge Cup and taking on the Presidency of Basingstoke Football Club. This was not untypical of the time, as the drinks trade, both brewers and publicans, was the earliest sponsor of organised sport, often providing grounds or dressing room accommodation, but John May's contribution was exceptional by any standards.

Lt. Col. John May – Basingstoke's Benefactor

The Old Pavilion

Basingstoke Cricket Club's first recorded match dates back to 1817, originally playing on the Common. Then "some years later a piece of ground known as the Folly, adjoining the Fairfields, was rented (to the Basingstoke club) for cricket, and here (in 1877) a rude pavilion was erected" (*Cricket in North Hants*, - J. May 1907). It is known that the

Folly was used for cricket from about the middle of the nineteenth century and it is thought possibly much longer than that. The ground at that time was significantly smaller than the one we know today and the square was positioned east-west rather than north-south. The "rude" pavilion was situated at the centre of the Castle Field boundary and was a single storey building constructed of timber with a thatched roof.

May's 'Bounty'

When the land had come up for sale in 1880 and the club was served notice to leave, John May had saved the day, managing to buy the land in order to preserve its use for sporting purposes. He had paid well above the market value in order to beat the property speculators at that time: the cost was £1,800 including the laying of a cinder cycle track. The name May's Bounty derived from a chance remark made at a club dinner the following year when Mr J. Lamb jokingly suggested it as a tribute to John May as the club's benefactor – and the new name caught on.

Bounty Road in Edwardian times showing the iron railings which fenced off the ground on the north side. Bounty road was originally named Back Lane.

It was a tribute to May's social connections that, to commemorate the beginning of his third tenure as President of the club in 1880 he was able to arrange a match between twenty-two of Basingstoke and district and the famous United South of England X1. This was a team which travelled all over the country playing cricket and for whom W.G. Grace had played for 'expenses' throughout the 1870s. On this occasion John May met the expenses of the team, some £80. The match was noteworthy for a sad event as, included in the United South of England X1 line-up was WG's brother and fellow

Gloucestershire player G.F. Grace – known as 'Fred' – who soon after died at the Red Lion Hotel at the tender age of 29, having caught a 'chill' after he took a swim on a fishing trip to the village of Andwell.

The New Pavilion

John May set in hand some improvements to the ground which were carried out at the turn of the century, enlarging it to its present size, demolishing the old pavilion and building a new one which, while it has since been much extended and modernised, remains the basis of the present pavilion. Interestingly the inscription on the plaque beneath the pavilion clock commemorates the inauguration of *the new century, January 1, 1901* which suggests that we may have been a little premature in celebrating the new century and millennium only 99 years later in the year 2000. The ground was largely re-turfed and the square was levelled and re-laid so that the wicket faced north-south, as now.

In July 1905 May presented the ground to the trustees on behalf of the club, which took over a 99 year lease at a nominal rent of £10 per annum "if demanded". By all accounts it was not often demanded. Years later, in 1950, the club was to buy the leasehold for just £450, making it one of the few clubs in Hampshire to own its ground.

A grand occasion at May's Bounty as Colonel May presents the ground to the club's trustees :1905

The first ever County match at Basingstoke was seen as an opportunity to popularise the game in the north of the county and there was much excitement around town at the prospect. Admission to the ground was 6d (six old pence) and to enclosures was 1s and 2s extra (1 and 2 shillings), but there were discounts available if tickets were purchased in advance from the "principal tradesmen of the town". Basingstoke at this time was a quiet market town of tree-lined streets with a population of 10,000, although the opening of the Thornycroft factory five years earlier had signalled the beginning of more industrial development.

Cricket as a Spectator Sport

England in the Edwardian period witnessed an upsurge of public awareness and interest in sport, particularly in football but also in cricket as evidenced by very large attendances at matches in metropolitan areas on Bank Holidays, such as the 80,000 at the Oval in this same year of 1906 to watch Surrey v. Yorkshire, two of the leading teams of the day. But such crowds were very much the exception and weaker counties such as Hampshire, relative newcomers to the County Championship in 1895, had smaller memberships and fewer supporters generally.

That this burgeoning interest in sport was shared by the people of Basingstoke, too, is indicated by the fervent and partisan support for the two main football clubs in the town at that time, Basingstoke and the North Hants Iron Works. John May had often despaired, however, that support for cricket in the town was sometimes fitful.

For the county game against Warwickshire there was encouragement for people to travel to the match from elsewhere in the county and beyond with cheap rail tickets available from stations on the South Western line and from Reading on the Great Western. Indeed railway travel played a key part in the popularisation of cricket as a spectator sport. But May's Bounty had been granted a match which ran from Monday to Wednesday. Most working people only had a half-day holiday on Saturday – and shop workers in Basingstoke on Thursday, the early closing day - which would largely have restricted the crowd to county members and the more leisured classes.

Also the *Gazette* recorded that the weather in late May was miserably cold throughout the match and that this affected the attendance, but it still felt that the gate was "decidedly encouraging". Similarly the *Daily Telegraph* considered that the Hampshire committee was making an "interesting experiment" in playing at Basingstoke and said that it was so cold on the first day that this would have deterred many from attending. John May in his book *Cricket in North Hants* wrote that there was a large attendance, and that financially the match proved a great success, so much so that it was expected that a County match at Basingstoke would become an annual event. All the arrangements had been made by the local club who also paid £75 expenses to the Hampshire team, after which the profit of £30 was shared equally by the Basingstoke and Hampshire clubs. But in the event May's Bounty was offered a less attractive fixture for the following season, against one of the weakest sides Northamptonshire at the end of May, which the Basingstoke committee declined (*Basingstoke and North Hants Cricket Club* - Harrison and Bichard, 1965).

They may have regretted this decision, since they had to wait until 1914 for their next opportunity.

HAMPSHIRE COUNTY Team at Basingstoke May 1906
Hopkins (Groundsman), Bowell, C.B. Llewellyn, Mead, Revd W.V. Jepson, Langford, F Bacon (Secretary);
E.M.C. Ede, Badcock, E.M. Sprot (Captain), Robson;
Capt. J.G. Greig and A.C. Johnston

[photo: courtesy of B&NHCC]

Hampshire – 1906

But what of this first Hampshire side to play at May's Bounty? They had suffered an incredibly poor run since the turn of the century, avoiding the wooden spoon only once (1901 when they finished joint seventh) in six seasons. The early County Championship had a curious point-scoring system. Initially points totals were calculated by deducting the number of losses from the number of wins. When the competition was expanded in 1895, each team had to play a minimum of 16 matches but the actual number of games played depended on how many each county could arrange, so in 1906 for example, Yorkshire played 28 while Hampshire only played 20. Positions in the table were determined by the number of points in finished games, excluding draws, expressed as a percentage of the number of finished games.

So Hampshire in 1906, in winning 7 but losing 9 matches had minus 2 points which as a % of 16 finished games came out at minus 12.5%. It sounds like they could have found work for Duckworth and Lewis!

To a large extent Hampshire's disastrous record at this time can be explained by the County's dependence on amateurs who were not consistently available - and particularly on soldiers who were not available at all around the Boer War period. They were an attractive side to watch as their amateur batsmen were famous for their extravagant strokeplay, but Hampshire lacked the bowling resources to bowl sides out. In 1905 Hampshire finished bottom yet had two batsmen (Captain J.G.Greig and A.J.L.Hill, both soldiers) in the top 8 batsmen in the national averages, while three batsmen, Greig, Hill and Llewellyn unusually all achieved the distinction of scoring a century in both innings of a match, respectively versus Worcestershire, Somerset, and Derbyshire.

A defining characteristic of Edwardian cricket was the class divide between gentlemen and players. Amateurs – usually boasting at least three initials to their names - enjoyed privileges such as first-class travel, separate dining rooms and dressing rooms, and even separate gates to the ground. They were addressed as 'Mr', while the professionals were simply addressed by surname, and the captain was always drawn from gentlemanly ranks. This was the age of glorious and uninhibited strokeplay, of superiority of bat over ball on featherbed wickets. Amateurs were usually batsmen – and also occupied the senior posts in cricket administration - and any proposals for rule changes to redress the balance a little in favour of the bowlers was firmly resisted, while bowling actions were closely scrutinised and a tight rein was kept on any bowler suspected of 'throwing'. Inevitably many matches ended in draws.

The distinction between amateurs and professionals was becoming blurred in some ways, notably in the remuneration received. The gentlemen seemed to make more from 'expenses' or from other sources such as sinecure jobs than the players did from the various elements which made up their legitimate income – match fees, 'talent money' (based on personal performances, for example a half-century or five wickets), win money and if they were lucky, winter pay and perhaps a benefit.

C. P. MEAD

Some counties, notably Yorkshire, were by now largely made up of professionals although weaker ones like Hampshire who lacked the resources to pay professionals still tended to have more amateurs. But this was beginning to change for the Hampshire side which was to take the field at May's Bounty. The trend towards a more professional balance began with players like Charles Llewellyn and Philip Mead. The South African Charles Llewellyn, a fine batsman and slow left-arm bowler – reputedly the first to bowl a 'chinaman' - had qualified for the county by residence and had already achieved the 'double' in his first season.

Then the young Philip Mead, failing to get a regular place in a very strong Surrey side, had similarly qualified for Hampshire and 1906 was his first full season. He was to go on to become one of the greatest of all left-handed batsmen, making 1,000 runs in a season 27 times and scoring an amazing 48,892 runs for the county, more than any other cricketer has ever scored for one club. Incredibly, when Hampshire returned to May's Bounty for the first time after World War 1, many years later in 1935, he was still in the side.

For Hampshire 1906 was to prove their best season for many years, rising to eighth place in the table. John Badcock was making a good impression as a much needed new fast bowler and he did as much as anyone to help Hampshire to turn things around. But there had been little evidence of this improvement early in the season and they came into the match at May's Bounty on the back of a 10-wicket defeat by Surrey. Warwickshire were one of the stronger county sides but they had also travelled up from a defeat at Taunton.

WARWICKSHIRE COUNTY Team at Basingstoke May 1906
Whittle, Charlesworth, Baker, George, Moorehouse, Smith, Kinneir;
Devey, Quaife, Lilley (Captain), Hargreave and Santall [photo: courtesy of B&NHCC]

Both Mead and Llewellyn were in the Hampshire team, captained by the wonderfully-named amateur batsman E.M. Sprot, for the May's Bounty fixture but neither was to leave his impression on the match. The star for Hampshire was Captain Greig who scored 79 and 98, took five wickets in Warwickshire's second innings, and made three catches - and yet finished on the losing side.

WILLS'S CIGARETTES.

WILLS'S CIGARETTES.

MR. E. M. SPROT (HAMPSHIRE).

A. A. LILLEY (WARWICKSHIRE).

THE CAPTAINS
[cards reproduced by kind permission of Imperial Tobacco Ltd, England]

Sixteen years later in 1922 Hampshire and Warwickshire were destined to play one of the most extraordinary matches in cricket history as Hampshire recovered from a first innings score of just 15 to win the match, scoring 521 following on, and then bowling Warwickshire out for 158 in the second innings. But this meeting at Basingstoke in 1906 earned a very minor footnote too. It would be difficult, however, for someone not steeped in cricket lore – and also perhaps for a young cricket follower today - to understand how this first match at Basingstoke came to be noted less for Warwickshire's victory than for the gentlemanly manner in which Hampshire lost.

The First County Match at May's Bounty

Hampshire had the best of the first day, dismissing Warwickshire for just 126 with the young fast medium bowler Langford taking four wickets. The Daily Telegraph reported that this was a feeble batting effort on a "dead pitch". The home side then reached 143 in losing only five wickets before the close, with Captain J. G. Greig 76 not out. Greig was a high class opening batsman who had first made his name playing cricket in India, but regrettably he was not always available due to his army commitments. He later had a spell as Hampshire County Cricket Club Secretary in the 1920s and eventually was ordained a Catholic priest and settled in the New Forest.

Hampshire failed to capitalise the following day, however, subsiding to 166 all out and then Warwickshire turned the game around with a substantial second innings score of 392 – never beaten since at May's Bounty -, with 171 coming from their stylish left-hand opening bat, Septimus Paul Kinneir. Kinneir, who was to make his Test debut for England at the age of 40 on the tour of Australia of 1911-12, obviously relished the Hampshire bowling since he was also to take a double century off them in 1911.

In this match at May's Bounty in 1906 Hampshire were left with the difficult task of scoring 353 to win in the fourth innings. Greig again batted superbly but he fell just short of his century, and with only the captain Sprot with 42 and the Reverend W. V. Jephson with 47 providing any significant support, Hampshire were all out for 245 and Warwickshire secured their victory by 107 runs.

HAMPSHIRE v. WARWICKSHIRE in progress at May's Bounty May 1906 *[photo: courtesy of B&NHCC]*

"Cricket … a Noble Heritage"

The attention of the cricket world was drawn to an otherwise unremarkable match, however, by the Warwickshire captain and England wicket-keeper A. A. Lilley, a famous figure amongst cricketers of the 'Golden Age'. He wrote to the *Daily Mail* to praise Hampshire's sportsmanship for batting on in rain when they had no chance of winning and would have been quite within their rights to have left the field. He wrote:

"In the rush and scurry of the County Championship, when everything is apt to be lost sight of, save, indeed the actual result, some of the old-fashioned courtesies of cricket are apt to be forgotten. Cricket…has been handed down to us – a noble heritage it is – by men who loved the game for itself….we should keep it pure and unsullied…..a game which will broaden the sympathies of the wealthy and raise the tone of those of humbler extraction who meet on a common level while they are on the pitch of green sward.

………to bat (in the rain) under these circumstances represents sportsmanship of the highest type, and on behalf of Warwickshire cricket I can assure Mr Sprot…that their action will be appreciated as long as the present generation of Warwickshire cricketers endures. Nor will the action be regretted by Hampshire. It is a spirit of this kind which makes cricket worth playing, and which I may say incidentally will make for its popularity."

While acknowledging that playing on in rain would not happen now with today's more mercenary approach, this does all seem way over the top. But it is very revealing. Even in this 'Golden Age' of cricket there was a feeling that some of the old values of sportsmanship were being lost and that cricket was becoming too humdrum. This was a cricketer, nearing the end of his playing days, looking back with nostalgia to the Victorian idyll – some would say myth - of cricket. This saw cricket as character-building – character of the sort which had won an Empire - and as instilling a code of behaviour which was quintessentially English and was to give to the English language such enduring notions as the 'straight bat', 'playing the game' and 'it's not cricket'.

Plaudits for May's Bounty

May's Bounty as a ground had come through its first County match very well. Well over 900 runs had been scored and it had seen its first first-class century and another individual score of 98. At a 'Smoking Concert' organised by Colonel May at the Drill Hall on Sarum Hill on the first evening of the match Arthur Lilley had paid tribute to the pretty ground and to the quality of the wicket which he felt could not have been bettered. This was a real tribute to Bert Butler who, appointed as groundsman in 1901, went on to devote himself for more than fifty years to May's Bounty and to the Basingstoke and North Hants Cricket Club as both groundsman and player. The Butler family is a notable one in the history of the club because his three sons also played with distinction for Basingstoke.

THE SCORES **May's Bounty 21, 22 and 23 May 1906**

Warwickshire 126 and 392 (Kinneir 171, George 71)

Hampshire 166 (Greig 79) and 245 (Greig 98)

<u>Warwickshire won by 107 runs</u>

A match between Basingstoke & North Hants and Hampshire in the 1900s *[photo: courtesy of B&NHCC]*

CHAPTER THREE

The 'Golden Age' Draws To a Close

World War I brought the 'Golden Age' of cricket to a close. But its glitter had tarnished somewhat well before 1914, as the County Championship became more competitive and professionals began to outnumber amateurs. Inevitably batsmen whose livelihood depended on their performance were less cavalier in their approach than the amateurs who had played with such freedom and panache. An article in the *Times* at the beginning of the 1914 season bemoaned the lack of "overwhelming personalities" like W.G. Grace and considered that first-class cricket had become "the dullest of games".

Financial Pressures

But the game as a whole was also in the early stages of a long and uncomfortable transition from its origins as a leisurely – if also financially rewarding - pursuit for gentlemen into an organised business enterprise. Association football had more appeal for working men since a ninety minute match leading to a definite result better suited the pattern of their lives which allowed only limited time for leisure. But attendances at first-class cricket matches were falling and a number of counties were having financial difficulties, to the extent that one or two were considering withdrawing from the competition. The Hampshire club had only a small membership (about 1,450) and was accumulating debts - and not just in wet summers like 1912. The following season, when attendances were regarded as good, still left them £200 in debt. The club had an increasing number of professionals on the payroll, had to pay for the upkeep of the ground at Southampton with its groundstaff, and in 1903 had appointed a salaried Club Secretary at £200 per annum. And on average each match, home and away, cost the club something like £160.

As for income, at that time it derived from money at the gate - the profit from matches was retained by the home club – , from members' subscriptions (about £1,650 per year), and from a share of the Test match pot which was not guaranteed but which might amount to £200 in a good year.

When war brought a break in county cricket Hampshire faced a deficit of £700. It was money problems, and the attempt to tackle them by mounting a membership campaign, which prompted another venture to bring first-class cricket to the north of the county in 1914. The club Secretary, F.H. Bacon, said that the club did not expect to cover its costs from the match arranged at Basingstoke but hoped to attract a nucleus of new members so as to justify an annual visit. The overall aim was to raise the membership to at least 2,000. Fred Bacon was a former Hampshire player, who had scored 114 in 130 minutes on his debut v. Warwickshire in 1894, and had originally played for the Basingstoke club. Sadly he was to lose his life in the war when the ship in which he was serving was sunk by a mine in 1915.

Hampshire - 1914

The Hampshire side which was to meet Derbyshire at May's Bounty in late May 1914 had made considerable strides since the county's first appearance at the ground eight years before. They had climbed to sixth place in the Championship in 1912 when the three leading batsmen in the national averages were all Hampshire players – the legendary C.B. Fry, who had joined the county in 1909, A.C Johnston (another of the highly talented soldier-batsman), and C.P. Mead who was by now an England player and a very prolific run scorer. That season they had achieved the rare feat – not repeated until Surrey's win in 1956 - of a county side beating the Australian touring side. The margin was eight wickets and Mead, a scourge to more than one Australian team in his time, scored 160 not out.

The HAMPSHIRE side which beat the Australians, 1912
E.R. Remnant, J. Stone, J. Newman, G.Brown, C.P.Mead, H. A.W. Bowell, A.S. Kennedy
G.N. Bignell, C.B. Fry, E.M. Sprot, E.I.M. Barratt, and Revd W.V. Jephson
[photo: courtesy of Hampshire County Cricket Club]

In 1913 they had fallen back and finished a disappointing tenth in the Championship – mainly due to a familiar problem, the frequent non-availability of their amateur batsmen. They now had a strong nucleus of professionals, however, who were to serve the County so well over the next twenty-five years and more. Among them were Alec Kennedy, Jack Newman, and George Brown. Kennedy bowled in-swingers and leg cutters and took nearly 3,000 wickets in his career, also completing the double five times, while Newman took over 2,000 wickets variously with off-spin and medium pace, achieving the double five times. Brown was a remarkably versatile and combative all-rounder – "at once a left-handed hitter, stone-waller, wicket-keeper, fast bowler, brilliant fielder and insatiable joker" (Altham, H. in *A History of Cricket*). Of the amateurs the future Hampshire captain the Hon. (later Lord) Tennyson – grandson of the Poet Laureate - had announced his arrival in 1913 with two fine hundreds and had won a last minute call-up for the MCC tour to South Africa.

Basingstoke had already enjoyed a glimpse of this newly emerging Hampshire side when a strong-looking county X1, appropriately captained by Fred Bacon, had visited May's Bounty in **1911** to play Eighteen of Basingstoke. Such matches preserved something of the tradition of social cricket characteristic of the Victorian era, whereby club cricketers could pit their skills against the best. The scorecard for that match was as follows:

Eighteen of Basingstoke

S.F. Allin c Stone b Brown	4	c Brown b Mead	8
Butler b Newman	21	b Mead	12
G.L. Rutherford lbw b Mead	0	lbw b Mead	1
A.R. Simpson c Smith b Mead	0	b Brown	10
A.P. Rutherford not out	73	c and b Brown	13
J.S. Rutherford b Newman	0	c and b Brown	17
F.B. Harvey b Mead	8	c and b Newman	18
L. Langdon c Mead b Kennedy	10	b Mead	15
G.T.B. Harvey b Mead	4	b Mead	14
T.R. White b Hopkins	1	st Stone b Bacon	6
R. Lamb b Brown	34	c Remnant b Brown	54
W.R.Hoare b Kennedy	4	b Bacon	13
H.W. Cobb b Kennedy	2	c Stone b Brown	3
A.C. Snow b Brown	8	b Kennedy	2
W.G. Hubbard b Newman	0	c Newman b Mead	4
G. Walter b Brown	3	b Mead	0
E.J. Searle c Fielder b Brown	0	c Mead b Kennedy	1
V.A.S. George b Newman	6	not out	0
Extras	9	Extras	6
	193		**197**

Hampshire

Stone b Snow	33	lbw b George	1
Kennedy lbw b Hoare	17	run out	23
Remnant run out	11	lbw b George	21
Mead b A.P. Rutherford	13	c Harvey b George	34
H.A.H. Smith b Snow	59	lbw b Snow	1
Brown lbw b A.P. Rutherford	14	lbw b A.P. Rutherford	1
Budden b Butler	0	b A.P. Rutherford	0
Newman not out	40	c Lamb b A.P. Rutherford	8
F.H. Bacon b A.P. Rutherford	3	not out	28
Fielder b Snow	2	lbw b Butler	0
Hopkins c Walter b A. Rutherford	0	run out	7
Extras	21	Extras	11
	213		**167**

Basingstoke won by ten runs
(From *A Celebration of 125 Years at May's Bounty*, B&NHCC 1990)

The brothers A.P. and J.S. Rutherford were both to make a few appearances for the full County side over the following two seasons.

One suggestion put forward in early 1914 at a meeting of members and supporters of Hampshire CCC at Basingstoke, called to discuss the need for increased membership, was for the county side to include a local player known to local supporters in the forthcoming match against Derbyshire. The player that they had in mind was Bert Butler who had twice achieved the double for Basingstoke. Unfortunately this plea fell on deaf ears.

London Street, BASINGSTOKE c. 1915

Hampshire had begun the 1914 season very strongly and came into the Derbyshire match on the back of a very creditable draw with the strong Yorkshire side at Southampton. Phil Mead had scored a superb 213 in a first innings score of 416. Meanwhile Derbyshire had beaten Nottinghamshire. Greig, Mead, and Sprot, who was captaining the side for the first time in the season, remained from the side of 1906.

Hampshire v. Derbyshire – 1914

Greig again found May's Bounty to his liking, treating the Basingstoke public to another great exhibition of strokeplay. He was, from contemporary accounts, regarded as the finest cutter in the English game. This time he reached the century he had narrowly been deprived of eight years earlier, as Hampshire posted 389 in reply to Derbyshire's first innings of 270, to secure a lead of 119. Phil Mead was the leading batsman for the county in 1914, and third in the national averages with 55 for each trip to the crease, but again May's Bounty was not to see the best of him.

ALEC BOWELL

It is interesting to note the scoring rates in the Gazette report of the match, perhaps allowing some licence for the reporter spicing up proceedings. Sprot in particular "scored with great rapidity by full shouldered drives, one mighty hit going right out of the ground…(and) with Newman he put on 127 runs in an hour." Greig's opening partner, the professional Alec Bowell in his benefit year, reached his half-century in 60 minutes, while in <u>rebuilding</u> (my emphasis) the Warwickshire innings after losing their first 4 wickets for just 24, Morton and Slater had added 191 runs in 130 minutes! Both narrowly missed centuries.

But the match very much belonged to a bowler, Arthur Jaques, an amateur who was a relative newcomer to the Hampshire team and whose very promising career was sadly to be cut short, killed in action on the Western Front the following year. He took 8 wickets for 67 in Derbyshire's first innings and followed up with 6 for 38 in their second innings of 200. This left Hampshire needing only 82 which they managed in just an hour's batting to complete an eight-wicket victory, their first win at the ground.

Jaques' match figures of 14 for 105 still stand as the first-class record for May's Bounty, while his first innings analysis has been beaten twice but only in very recent years – by Kevan James' 8-49 in 1997 and by Peter Hartley's 8-65 in 1999. Tall and loose-limbed, Jaques was one of the first exponents of 'leg theory' bowling, right arm in-swing at fast-medium pace mixed with occasional cutters and delivered from an awkward height. He bowled around the wicket with a ring of close fielders on the leg side. This was the tactic which, when executed at much faster pace by Larwood, was to cause such controversy in the 'Bodyline' series in Australia in 1933. At the end of the season Jaques was selected for the Gentlemen v. the Players at Lords, an honour probably more prized in those days than winning a Test cap, and he took this same approach into that match under the captaincy of C.B. Fry. It is testimony to Jaques' success in 1914 that his haul of wickets at May's Bounty did not prove to be his best of the season – he later took 14 Somerset wickets for 53 at Bath. All told he finished with 112 wickets at 18 apiece.

THE SCORES **May's Bounty 27, 28 and 29 May 1914**
Derbyshire 270 (Slater 99, Morton 96, Jaques 8-67) and 200 (Slater 38, Morton 36, Jaques 6-38)
Hampshire 389 (Greig 100, Sprot 87, Newman 55, Cadman 6-94) and 84-2 (Greig 33 not out)   <u>Hampshire won by eight wickets</u>

Hampshire went on to finish fifth in the County Championship, their best to date. The match at May's Bounty had proved a very satisfactory one for all concerned in the home camp. Despite Jaques' exceptional individual success with the ball, there was plenty of good batting with one century and two scores in the nineties, and Hampshire had achieved a fine win. The home side's performance had increased the gate which on the second day reached well over 1,500, doubtless boosted after lunch by shop workers enjoying their half-holiday on early closing day. In 1914, in an effort to improve attendance, first-class matches had been programmed for the first time to begin on Saturdays and Wednesdays.

But consideration of future venues proved to be academic as world events intervened in early August 1914 and, even when first-class cricket resumed five years later, it was to be many years before Basingstoke was to see another match. During the war years May's Bounty largely fell into disuse and became overgrown with weeds.

C.B. FRY in his Hampshire days

BETWEEN THE WARS

CHAPTER FOUR

The 1920s: Hampshire 'Club and Ground' at May's Bounty

"Basingstoke….bloody tiny little ground…..wonderful day….nice chaps"

After the war B&NHCC faced an enormous task to bring May's Bounty back to its former condition. All the weeding was carried out painstakingly by hand and at that time even mowers and rollers were only horse and man-powered (Harrison and Bichard). But the Basingstoke club managed to prepare itself in time for a full season of fixtures in 1919.

BASINGSTOKE c. 1921

Counties, too, faced difficulties in preparing to resume the county cricket programme and an unsuccessful experiment of two-day Championship matches was tried. But in the post-war period attendances picked up dramatically as crowds, starved of sporting entertainment, flocked to cricket and football matches. This, despite the fact that admission prices to both rose from the pre-war 6d to one shilling. County cricket also benefited from the fine weather in 1919. Hampshire's membership had grown to 2,613 by 1923 but this level was not to be sustained despite various membership campaigns. By 1938 it had fallen to 2,000 but then rose to 2,600 again in 1939, the highest for ten years.

Although the Hampshire club had managed to clear most of its debts by the end of the war as some members had agreed to continue to pay their subscription fees, the inter-war years proved to be years of mounting debts for Hampshire and most other county clubs. In the 1920s the club concentrated on purchasing shares in the County Ground Company, a company which had been formed in 1893 and which owned the freehold of the Northlands ground. In 1927 it also formed a company to take over the lease of the Dean Park ground at Bournemouth. Inevitably perhaps the focus centred exclusively on the south of the county and in fact no first-class cricket was seen north of Southampton between 1914 and 1935.

Hampshire 'Club and Ground'

In the meantime Basingstoke had to be satisfied with visits from Hampshire Club and Ground sides. But happily these often amounted virtually to the full county team. All counties ran such teams primarily as a feeder to the county club but also to foster cricket in the county, to discover new talent, and to find new members. One visit by Hampshire Club and Ground to May's Bounty stands out, partly because the Hampshire team was at the height of its fame and partly because the match was witnessed by John Arlott as a 'Basingstoke boy' – and later vividly recalled.

The year was 1921, a year when Hampshire, with a clutch of great players but not quite a great team and rising only to sixth place in the Championship, nevertheless came to national prominence as never before. The reason was the heroic performance of the three Hampshire players – Tennyson, Mead and Brown - called to England colours to do battle with Gregory and McDonald, the fearsome Australian quick bowlers who were cutting a swath through English batsmen both in the county matches and in the Test series. Tennyson was called up for the second Test and performed so well that he was appointed captain of the ailing England side for the third. He picked up a nasty hand injury while fielding and needed three stitches. But nothing was going to prevent him taking his place in the batting line-up. He had to bat virtually one-handed and yet incredibly scored fifty in an hour's play, finishing with 63. The innings captured the imagination of the English public. This was heroism worthy of the pen of his grandfather Alfred, Lord Tennyson, the Victorian Poet Laureate whose verse had immortalised the *Charge of the Light Brigade*. Doubtless to Lionel this was his 'Valley of Death' as he faced 'Aussies to the left of him, Aussies to the right of him'.

P. MEAD   HON. L. H. TENNYSON (Captain).   G. BROWN

HAMPSHIRE AND ENGLAND.

[Photo reproduced by kind permission of 'The Cricketer']

George Brown was another who thrived on adversity and, while not even the regular Hampshire wicket-keeper, he was selected to keep wicket and open the batting for England. He too took on the Australian quicks in exciting fashion, often driving straight over the bowler's head. And Phil Mead, who scored 3,000 runs that season and had already made a century against the Australians for Hampshire, scored 182 not out in the final Test at the Oval, which until 1938 remained the highest score ever played for England against Australia in this country.

Mead had a - sometimes deserved - reputation as a stodgy batsman. On one occasion in a county match Tennyson lost patience with him and had a telegram delivered to Mead at the wicket which read "Too boring. Get out immediately!" But here on the big occasion he added 121 for the sixth wicket in 100 minutes with Tennyson, with his cavalier captain only contributing 51. In the morning session, two and a half hours play, Mead scored 109 runs. Tennyson played in four tests that year, Brown three and Mead two, and they occupied three of the four top places in the England batting averages.

P.MEAD G. BROWN

HAMPSHIRE AND ENGLAND.

[Photo reproduced by kind permission of 'The Cricketer']

And after such derring-do here at the end of the season were all three heroes at May's Bounty in the Club and Ground side to play Fifteen of Basingstoke. In front of reportedly the largest crowd ever packed into the ground Basingstoke batted first and had the temerity to declare, having lost only 12 of their wickets, and left Hampshire 254 to win. Mead suffered his customary failure at May's Bounty and Brown hit some characteristic drives but it was what followed that left a deep impression on the young John Arlott as Tennyson cut loose, in an innings of thundering aggression as the ball was bludgeoned to all parts of the ground and beyond. He was eventually caught for 169, with five sixes and 24 fours. The required runs were made in just 80 minutes, but Hampshire batted on to complete the entertainment and had scored 308 for 7 in just over two hours by the end of play.

After the game, the ground was illuminated and there was dancing to the music of the North Hants Iron Works Band (Harrison and Bichard). Prompted to remember the match some twenty-five years later by John Arlott, the larger than life Tennyson recalled:

"Basingstoke, wemember it distinctly, dear boy: bloody tiny little ground, though; sixes pwetty easy. Wonderful day; gweat party afterwards; nice chaps…" (Article in the *Observer* quoted in *The Essential John Arlott* – David Rayvern Allen ed. 1989).

HAMPSHIRE.
Left to right, back row: –Livsey, Kennedy, Bowell, Newman, R. Aird. Brown,
Front Row: –H. S. Altham, A. L. Hosie, Hon. L.H. Tennyson (Captain), H.C. McDonell, Mead.

[Photo reproduced by kind permission of 'The Cricketer']

For a while these matches became almost an annual event. When Hampshire Club and Ground returned in 1922 it was a fine bowler, Alec Kennedy, who performed the greatest feat, taking 6 for 16, including a hattrick, as Basingstoke were all out for 127, Butler top scoring with 42. This was hardly a surprise, however, in a season in which Kennedy had taken 177 first-class wickets at just 16 apiece. In fact he and Newman shared an amazing total of 340 wickets, while no other Hampshire player took as many as 40.

The Club and Ground replied with 148 and on this occasion Mead did score runs at May's Bounty, although his score of 63 only matched his first-class average for the season in which he had amassed 2,265 runs.

This match was a considerable success, the gate realising the substantial sum of over £100, and again there was entertainment provided on the ground afterwards.

H. L. V. DAY.
(HANTS)

H.L.V. DAY –
soldier-cricketer and England rugby
international

*[photo reproduced by kind permission of
'The Cricketer']*

Kennedy was rewarded by a tour to South Africa in 1922-23 along with three other Hampshire players Mead, Newman, and Livsey who served Tennyson not only as a wicket-keeper but had also acted as his valet in the war. A fifth, H.L.V. Day – Hampshire's latest soldier-batsman and also an English international rugby three-quarter – had to decline his invitation due to his army commitments. Although a number of the prominent players in England opted out of the tour, this was still some testament to the strength of the Hampshire team at this time.

Two years later there was excitement in Basingstoke at the prospect of seeing Lionel Tennyson make hay once more, but he failed to appear with the Club and Ground side as expected. But May's Bounty still had the considerable treat of seeing four other England players – Mead, Brown, Livsey, and Kennedy.

Overall the Hampshire County team perhaps under performed in terms of Championship results but they remained one of the strongest counties for most of the 1920s, while never climbing above the 6th place they achieved in the 1921 and 1922 seasons.

  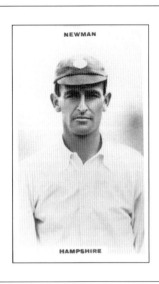

CHAPTER FIVE

The 1930s: County Cricket Returns to May's Bounty

Hampshire in the Thirties

When first-class cricket returned to May's Bounty in the 1930s the Basingstoke public was to see a quite different Hampshire team. By 1935 the group of wonderful players who had first come together for Hampshire before the First World War and who had graced their cricket in the 1920s, had all but disappeared. Of the leading professionals Brown, Kennedy, Newman and Livsey had all retired, although Kennedy played in August when on holiday from his coaching appointment at Cheltenham College. Only Phil Mead, incredibly at age forty-eight, still remained and he was to top the Hampshire averages yet again in 1935. He was the only survivor of the two previous first-class games at May's Bounty and he still had two further appearances to make there.

There were changes too in Hampshire's amateur ranks. Of the 1920s side, only Tennyson, now Lord Tennyson, remained and he was now playing less frequently. County cricket generally, from the playing perspective at least, was now clearly dominated by professionals and, with the exception of two wins for Middlesex just after the war, the Championship was monopolised by the northern counties, particularly Yorkshire. The leading batsmen of the inter-war years were professionals – from Hobbs and Hendren through to Hammond and Hardstaff, and latterly to Hutton and Compton. Apart from the cavalier Compton perhaps, these were not the artists of years gone by but batsmen of a different stamp – magnificent players but more efficient, calculating, and content to play the percentages.

But essentially little had changed in the way cricket was organised and structured, despite the fact that three-day cricket was poorly attended and counties continued to struggle financially. There was still an in-built resistance to professionals taking on the captaincy and Wally Hammond had to become an amateur before he could captain the England side. There were various discussions about how to improve cricket as a spectacle, but only minor modifications resulted – such as a slightly smaller ball which was easier for bowlers to grip, a slight enlargement of the wicket, and a change to the lbw law to reduce the negative pad play which had become so prevalent.

The second decade of the inter-war period was a disappointing one for the Hampshire team which for the most part occupied the lower half of the county table. Attempts to introduce a two-division Championship had been resisted in the past, but the relative playing strengths of the counties meant that, effectively, there was already a two-tier competition. Hampshire was now firmly in the lower tier with the likes of Northamptonshire, Worcestershire, Glamorgan and Somerset.

W.G.L.F. Lowndes, a gifted all-round cricketer, had assumed the Hampshire captaincy. He was an Etonian and, like most amateurs, was not available as often as the County would have liked and as many as four other amateurs captained the side at various times during 1935. Of the new breed of professionals, key players were Arnold, McCorkell, and Herman.

PLAYER'S CIGARETTES

J. ARNOLD (HAMPSHIRE)

PLAYER'S CIGARETTES

N. McCORKELL

[cards reproduced by kind permission of Imperial Tobacco Ltd, England]

Worthy though they were they could not quite match those they had replaced. John Arnold was a rarity – a double international in cricket and soccer. An attractive opening batsman, he had already won his solitary Test cap in 1931, had scored over 2,000 runs in 1934 and was to go on to score 1,000 runs in a season fourteen times. Neil McCorkell was a very consistent wicket-keeper over nineteen seasons and made himself into a more than useful opening partner for Arnold. He came close to Test selection and was to go on the tour to India with Lord Tennyson's side in 1937-38. 'Lofty' Herman was an opening bowler who took over 1,000 wickets for the County.

HAMPSHIRE CCC 1936
J. Arnold, E. Pothecary, H. Lawson,O. Herman, W. Creese, E. Drake, G. Hill
N. McCorkell, A. Baring, R. Moore (Capt), P. Mead and G. Boyes
(Note the inclusion of Ted Drake, famous centre-forward for Southampton, Arsenal and England, complete with central hair-parting. He played 16 first-class matches for Hampshire, 1931-36)

Basingstoke Prepares to Host the County Team Once More

The announcement in January **1935** that Hampshire was to play a county match at May's Bounty in June that year for the first time in twenty-one years caused much interest in the town. There was a great deal of civic pride in Basingstoke and the May's Bounty ground was considered to be one of its prize assets. The Mayor Harry Goodall appreciated the importance of the return to the town of the County team and he certainly pulled out all the stops to make it a success. The fixture was with neighbours Surrey so it held out the potential of a good attendance. He stressed to the local residents and tradespeople the importance of the town making a good impression on the many visitors. At his suggestion the main streets were decorated on the three days of the match with flags and bunting – left over from the King George V and Queen Mary's Silver Jubilee celebrations earlier in June - and this created a real sense of occasion. He also appealed for more local people to become county members. At the match a marquee was erected near the pavilion, decorated with flowers, and it was a jolly scene as the Mayoress later entertained her invited guests to tea.

Harry Goodall received a number of offers of help with match arrangements, including a Mrs G.J. Lansley who provided free use of the field adjoining the ground for car parking, which was supervised by the Automobile Association. Basingstoke Football Club allowed refreshment tents to be erected in Castle Field, at that time their home ground, on the south side of the ground. Mr J. Colman (of Colman's Mustard), who was a member of the Surrey County Cricket Club committee, offered to put up some of the Surrey players and their wives for two nights at Malshanger Park – interestingly an offer confined to the amateur players Percy Fender, the former England player, and Monty Garland-Wells, a gifted all-round sportsman who also had to his credit an England amateur football cap won as a goal-keeper. Fender was one of the real characters of the period, an all-rounder who had once scored a hundred in 35 minutes and an exceptional and unorthodox captain, but he had given up the captaincy of Surrey in 1931.

P.G.H. FENDER –
a legendary and
idiosyncratic
figure in the history of cricket

The Hampshire club had been lobbied on many occasions to bring first-class cricket back to the north of the county but they pointed out that there were additional expenses in playing matches away from headquarters. However they had finally agreed to the request and had held out the prospect of a regular yearly fixture if the match was a success. Receipts of £170 over the three days were suggested as an acceptable benchmark.

In the event the match, a weekday game scheduled for Wednesday to Friday, drew an estimated 2,000 spectators on the first day and 1,500 on the second. But unfortunately – through no fault of the May's Bounty wicket – the match was all over by the second afternoon. This did not prevent Basingstoke being granted its much sought-after annual fixture each year up until 1938, indeed Hampshire appeared twice at the ground in 1937. Regrettably the outcome was a succession of defeats, some quite heavy. Overall this seems to have reflected on the home county's poor batting rather than on the quality of the wickets prepared by Bert Butler.

Hampshire v. Surrey - 1935

1935 was a wet summer and the day before the Surrey match had seen a heavy storm and, when the Hampshire captain Lowndes made the perhaps surprising decision to bat first, the home side collapsed to 79 all out before lunch! The Surrey and (later) England fast bowler Alf Gover did the damage, getting some awkward bounce from the wicket helped by his extreme height. He was a good new ball bowler, with late away swing and a break-back ball in his armoury, and he had four victims bowled or caught at the wicket.

Surrey fared much better when they batted, passing Hampshire's score without loss. The first wicket was an lbw decision under the new experimental rule – under which the batsman could be out even if the ball pitched outside the off stump – which had been introduced to combat excessive pad play and, in the interests of brighter cricket, to reduce the supremacy of bat over ball. But the main interest in Surrey's innings of 274 was that the former England opener Andrew Sandham, who for so many years had formed a famous opening partnership with Jack Hobbs, emulated Hobbs' achievement and reached his hundredth hundred. This was a landmark he was happy to recall when he returned to May's Bounty as Surrey's scorer in 1966. Sandham, neat and dapper, was an attractive batsman who excelled in the cut and hook and he was the sole survivor of the long line of outstanding batsmen who had made Surrey such a strong side both before and after the First World War - among them the incomparable Hobbs, and the likes of Hayward, Abel and Jardine.

Hampshire batted with more resolution the second time around on a drying wicket and at times in poor light, with Arnold making 56 and Mead 32, but they could not make Surrey bat again nor take the game into the third day, losing by an innings and 7 runs.

They went on to finish the 1935 a disappointing second from bottom, having used as many as 28 different players during the season as well as the five amateur captains, not a recipe for success. The following season, however, was a much more encouraging one, even if the early form of a younger team could not be sustained. They came to Basingstoke in early July **1936** as the only undefeated county in the country and their opponents were Nottinghamshire, one of the strongest teams in the Championship, who boasted an opening attack of the body-line pairing, Larwood and Voce, and one of England's premier stroke-players of the inter-war years, Joe Hardstaff (Junior). They as a club had become embroiled in the politicking which followed the bodyline controversy and neither bowler had played for England since. Hampshire, however, had already to their cost run into Larwood and Voce at their best the year before, subsiding to 37 all out in their second innings to lose by a mammoth innings and 241 runs! The omens were not good.

Hampshire were now captained by R. H. Moore, an enterprising captain and an attacking batsman who in 1937 was to score a remarkable 316 in 380 minutes against Warwickshire, still the highest score ever made for the County. Phil Mead was in his last season and remarkably had completed his 150th first-class century. For the first time in many years the Basingstoke crowd was to see one of its own in Hampshire colours, the Basingstoke and North Hants fast medium bowler Howard Lawson who was to take 50 wickets for the County in 1936.

Hampshire v. Nottinghamshire - 1936

Lawson went wicket-less in his appearances in first-class cricket on his home ground, but he had the satisfaction of hitting Voce for a six in this game. Doubtless his inclusion in the team for the 1936 match boosted the crowd, which numbered just short of 3,000 by the afternoon session on the first day and over 2,000 on the second day of play. Stuart Boyes, who gave the County good service as a left-arm spinner and excellent short-leg fielder in this inter-war period, had opted for this game as a benefit match and a collection for him on the first day realised £23.

STUART BOYES – left-arm spinner, short-leg fielder, and stubborn lower order batsman
[photo reproduced by kind permission of 'The Cricketer']

The game against Nottinghamshire, however, followed a very similar pattern to the defeat by Surrey. Dick Moore opted to bat after heavy overnight rain on the uncovered strip had delayed the start and Hampshire were bowled out for 107, McCorkell top-scoring with 34. Harold Larwood bowling down the hill at May's Bounty must have been a fearsome sight, even though he was now content to bowl at three-quarter speed. His action retained its classic beauty – to all except the facing batsman - and he still achieved pace off the wicket as well as late swing with the new ball. But on this occasion he was hindered by damp footholds and he needed copious amounts of sawdust and was content with short spells, nevertheless still taking 2-7. It was Voce, fast medium left-arm, who was the most successful taking 4-21 while under the watchful eye of a Test selector.

HAROLD LARWOOD who bowled at May's Bounty in 1936

The wicket had eased somewhat when Nottinghamshire went in to bat and they had almost reached the Hampshire score for the loss of only two wickets by the end of the first day. The second day was washed out, but they still had plenty of time because they were able to declare at 215-7 and then needed just one hour and three-quarters to bowl Hampshire out again for 61. Voce took 6-37 – latterly with leg-breaks - and it helped him to get his England place back, but the Daily Telegraph commented on the "lack of resolution" in the batting.

Hampshire soon returned to form, however, winning four of their next six matches and, despite a poor end to the season, finished a creditable tenth in the Championship table.

Being awarded two county matches for **1937** was triumph indeed for Basingstoke. Cambridge University were the first opponents in July for a match running from Saturday to Tuesday. The first day was brilliantly sunny and attracted a shirt-sleeved crowd of over 2,000, of whom 1,772 paid at the gate. On Monday, again a sunny day, the gate was 1,086 but on the third day it was cold and overcast and only 373 paid at the gate to see Cambridge win a close-fought game. Receipts for the match totalled £173.

Hampshire v. Cambridge University - 1937

Oxford and Cambridge Universities in those days provided the counties with much stiffer opposition than is the case today and often had budding England players in their ranks. On this occasion the Cambridge team was captained by the future Yorkshire and England captain and all-rounder Norman Yardley. He later had the dubious distinction of captaining England against the all-conquering Australian side of 1948, which was every bit as formidable as their predecessors of 1921. The way that he was outmanoeuvred by Don Bradman's harder approach made the England selectors for the first time start to question the wisdom of recruiting their captains only from the available amateurs.

The University's batting was opened by the bespectacled Paul Gibb, another Test player in the making, a wicket-keeper-batsman and also a future umpire. Both Gibb and Yardley made big contributions to the University's win, Gibb scoring 113 in the first innings and Yardley a well-paced 64 not out in the second to guide them to victory. Yardley also took nine wickets in the match with his swing bowling. Hampshire had begun the match well with Arnold – in a very good run of form at this time - entertaining the crowd with an innings of 172 made in 155 minutes - the highest first-class score made to date at May's Bounty. Lawson contributed an entertaining knock of 29, to the evident delight of his home crowd. But Hampshire's score of 316 was easily overhauled by the University's 461, with Pawle as well as Gibb scoring a century, and the home side could only score 285 the second time around. Cambridge had some difficulty in the fourth innings but managed to get home by 3 wickets with ten minutes to spare.

It was reassuring for Bert Butler to be able to demonstrate that the May's Bounty wicket, provided with the good weather that had been denied to his work of preparation in recent seasons, could last for three days and host a high-scoring game with three centurions. The *Gazette* reported that the wicket showed no signs of wear even on the last day and that County Cricket Club officials had expressed themselves very satisfied with it.

Hampshire v. Leicestershire - 1937

It was a familiar story in the second match in August 1937, however, as poor Hampshire batting led to a win for Leicestershire by nine wickets in two days, which turned out to be their only success of the summer. The Basingstoke public again turned out in good numbers in fine weather, over 2,000 paying on the first day – a Saturday - to see Leicestershire bat all day on a good wicket to reach 404. Leslie Berry, the mainstay of their batting at this time, reached his 2,000 runs for the season and scored 153 on the day. Their most famous player, George Geary, the veteran former England fast-medium bowler, took a wicket in each innings and scored 26. For Hampshire Herman toiled manfully to finish with 5-124. The Hampshire first innings was something of a procession and at 180 all out they were asked to follow on. Of the front-line batsmen only McCorkell performed, making 50, and it was only a stand of 92 in 50 minutes late in the innings between Herman and Creese, which saved another innings defeat. As it was Leicestershire completed the job on the Monday evening, losing one wicket for 32 facing the unusual opening bowling combination of Arnold and McCorkell. Only Herman of the Hampshire players could look back on the game with satisfaction. His 91 not out –

following his 57 in the Cambridge match – confirmed his liking for the May's Bounty ground. He only exceeded this score once – and then by just one run - in a career spanning nineteen years.

Another special occasion at May's Bounty during 1937 was a ladies' two-day match between the West of England and the visiting Australian Women's Cricket Test team. The *Gazette* records that the attendance was scarcely less than the usual county gate and that the Mayor used the occasion to entertain to tea "members of county families and some of the principal residents of the town". The touring side won by eight wickets with Miss P. Holmes scoring a double century before retiring, which was a record score by an Australian lady player at that time. Only three wickets fell to bowlers during the tourists' first innings of 342-5 dec. but all three were to Miss Myson of the Sherfield-on- Loddon Ladies' Cricket Club.

VISIT OF THE AUSTRALIAN WOMEN'S CRICKET TEST TEAM

[Photo: H. A. Aylward, Basingstoke.

AUSTRALIAN WOMEN'S TEST TEAM v. WEST OF ENGLAND WOMEN AT MAY'S BOUNTY, BASINGSTOKE.

[photo: courtesy of Gazette Newspapers]

Hampshire v. Worcestershire - 1938

*It was business as usual it seemed when Hampshire returned to May's Bounty in May **1938** but at least this time they took the game into the third day. Worcestershire declared at their overnight second innings score of 228 for 9 (Sid Buller, another who like Gibb was to become a famous and controversial Test Match umpire, top-scoring with 50) and set Hampshire 301 to win on the final morning. To the disappointment of the home crowd they saw yet another collapse and Worcestershire won by 193 runs. Hampshire had shown more resistance in the first innings, mainly due to a late order stand of 129 between Boyes and Hill, who scored 46 not out and 77 respectively. This still remains a first-class record at the ground for the eighth wicket. All twenty Hampshire wickets had* *been shared by the pace bowlers Perks and Martin and they had bowled unchanged throughout the second innings. A plus point for Hampshire was the fast bowling of the Reverend J.W.J. Steele, who took five wickets in the Worcestershire first innings. He was an Army chaplain and regrettably this severely restricted his appearances. Also the reliable pace bowler George Heath took eight wickets in the match in this his most successful season for the club. One other point of interest with hindsight is that Henry Horton's elder brother Joseph was in the Worcestershire side for this match.*

May's Bounty was not granted a county fixture the following year and R. C. Brooks, the Basingstoke and North Hants Secretary who had made all the arrangements for the previous match, resigned from the County Committee and Basingstoke withdrew its affiliation with the Hampshire club. The weather had not been kind to Bert Butler in his preparation of the wicket for the match in 1938, as on a number of other occasions in the 1930s, but it would have been harsh to lay the blame for Hampshire's failure at his door. In fact it was a not untypical performance of a very 'in and out' season for Hampshire, with nine wins to their credit but sixteen defeats and only five draws. Nor, however, does it seem to have been an untypical May's Bounty wicket for the late 1930s because when Basingstoke met the Hampshire Club and Ground in 1939 they bowled them out for 26 and then in reply scored only 44 themselves.

HAMPSHIRE CCC 1939
N.T. McCorkell, L. Harrison, G.E.M. Heath, D.F. Walker, A.G. Holt, J. Arnold, G. Hill, J. Bailey
A.E. Pothecary, G.R. Taylor (capt), G.S. Boyes, and W.L. Creese
[photo: courtesy of Hampshire County Cricket Club]

THE EARLY POST-WAR
PERIOD

CHAPTER SIX

May's Bounty in the Wilderness

In 1945 the May's Bounty ground was in much better shape than it had been after World War 1 as the Basingstoke and North Hants club had continued to play matches there during the war. But May's Bounty was to be denied any Championship cricket in the twenty years following the war, the one first-class match being a visit by Oxford University in 1951. The 'post-war austerity' affecting England in the late forties and fifties also extended in Basingstoke, it seemed, to first-class cricket which was rationed as severely as any other basic 'commodity'.

There were some interesting games played there, nevertheless, in the immediate post-war period, notably appearances in 1946 and 1947 by Jim Sim's Middlesex X1 against XV of Basingstoke, the second of which attracted over 4,000 spectators to see the Compton brothers, Denis and Leslie, and other star performers. This was the gloriously sunny summer when Denis Compton and Bill Edrich scored mountains of runs, Compton hitting 3,816 and averaging over 90 with eighteen centuries. At May's Bounty he was c. Holloway b. A. Butler for a modest 43, but it was scored in just 15 minutes!

Jim Sims leads out his Middlesex X1 v. Basingstoke & North Hants, August 1947
[photo: courtesy of B&NHCC]

club, played the Club and Ground once more. In 1948 a Basingstoke XV entertained a County side again for the benefit of Hampshire players Herman, Arnold, Hill, McCorkell and Bailey. Because of the years lost to the war, a joint benefit had been awarded to these five, now senior, professionals to extend over the three years 1948 to 1950. It was hoped to raise at least £1,000 for each player, a target to which this game contributed £200.

Two years later in **1950** May's Bounty was to see the celebrated West Indian Test players, Frank Worrell, Prior Jones and Jeff Stollmeyer, not as players but as spectators – on a rest day from the Test Match at the Oval – at a match between Basingstoke and the West Indian Wanderers. This attracted over 2,000 people and they saw Jewell and Harman, in the words of the *Gazette*, "do a Ramadhin and Valentine" in spinning out the Wanderers for 69. The home side only managed to win by two wickets, however, and a second time-limited match was then played with a similar result.

TEST CRICKETERS AT THE FOLLY

Jeff Stollmeyer, Prior Jones, and Frank Worrell, West Indian Test cricketers, with John Arlott at May's Bounty, 1950
[photo: courtesy of Gazette Newspapers]

In July 1950 E.D.R. Eager's County team beat X11 of Basingstoke by 62 runs, with " a young and enterprising lad, Peter Sainsbury " taking three wickets and Fred Butler top-scoring with 55 for the town team.

The full scorecard for that match was:

E.D.R. Eager's X1

N. McCorkell run out	28
D. McCorkell b Harman	6
A.W.H. Rayment st Wills b Jewell	41
O.W. Herman b Jewell	3
G. Hill not out	62
J. Bailey st Wills bJewell	14
R. Pitman c Butler b Harman	11
N.H. Rodgers not out	6
Extras	8
(for 6 wickets dec)	179

Jewell 3-70
Harman 2-49

X11 of Basingstoke

F. Butler st N. McCorkell b Herman	55
R. Harrison c Pitman b Heath	0
G. Jewell c Bailey b Sainsbury	10
A. Wills b Herman	8
H.M. Lawson c Bailey b Sainsbury	0
W. Pocock c Rogers b Sainsbury	0
P. Holloway b Debnam	12
R. Smith st N. McCorkell b Bailey	5
J. Harman b Debnam	6
P. Bryant not out	1
F. Kempster c Eager b Bailey	1
H. Wing st McCorkell b Herman	3
Extras	9
	117

Sainsbury 3-36
Herman 3-23

There were Hampshire second XI fixtures at May's Bounty too. In the 1950 Minor Counties match versus Middlesex second X1, there was local interest in that Basingstoke players Guy Jewell and Fred Butler were making their county debuts. Both performed extremely well, Butler making the second highest score of 68 and Jewell taking 7-100 in the match as Hampshire won by ten wickets. Both were selected to play against Kent at May's Bounty the following year but Jewell had to withdraw with an injury. Guy Jewell was an outstanding club cricketer for a period of over thirty years, taking 1,820 wickets for

Basingstoke at 10 runs apiece and making over 10,000 runs. Had he chosen to make cricket rather than teaching his profession he could well have provided good back-up to Charles Knott and Jim Bailey in the County's spin department before Sainsbury arrived on the scene. As it was his first-class career was limited to one match for Hampshire against Glamorgan at Swansea in 1952, in which he was caught off Wilf Wooller for nought in the first innings and run out for one in the second. He had match bowling figures of 1-52 and he held two catches. He also played for the Club Cricket Conference X1. He was a rarity in club cricket, a big spinner of the ball who interspersed his stock chinaman deliveries with occasional orthodox left-arm spin.

The Hampshire 2nd XI team who played Middlesex 2nd XI at May's Bounty last week. F. T. Butler and C. A. Jewell, who were in the Hampshire team, are second and third from right respectively.

Hampshire 2nd X1 leaving the field in the match v. Middlesex 2nd X1 – 1950
[photo: courtesy of Gazette Newspapers]

County cricket after the war had entered a period in which it struggled to re-establish its relevance. In many areas of life war sometimes proves to be the stimulus for change. Not so, it proved, for first-class cricket which for the next fifteen years or so seemed to be locked in a time warp. This despite some obvious signals for change, such as the great success of one-day games during the war. Initially public relief at the end of war brought an upsurge in interest in cricket but it soon became clear that the three day game had lost much of its appeal. Attendances fell by fifty per cent in the next ten years. In 1951 15 of the 17 counties suffered a financial loss, if shares of Test Match receipts are discounted. Hampshire's loss of £820 was one of the smallest. The Championship was completely dominated by Surrey, who won it seven years in a row in the 1950s and whose team-sheet read rather like the England line-up. Their second string, called into constant action with the number of Test calls made on the leading players like May, Bedser, Laker and Lock, was still good enough to maintain the County's position of dominance even in their absence. County cricket, however, became a rather turgid affair with the proportion of matches which were drawn rising once more to around fifty per cent. Various contributory factors were being debated at the time – wickets were now covered 24 hours before play and were regarded as too easy paced, defensive field placings were being employed, and slow scoring was producing stalemate situations.

Meanwhile for Hampshire E.D.R. Eager had enthusiastically assumed the twin roles of captain and Secretary after the war and in 1949 Arthur Holt found his niche as county coach. This was the partnership which – albeit slowly - laid the foundations of the side which, after Colin Ingleby-Mackenzie succeeded Eager as captain, was to rise to second place in 1958 and to lift the Championship trophy for the first time in 1961. The County had of necessity to cultivate its young talent and – after some difficult times, second to bottom in 1947 and 1949 - there were some signs by 1951 that it was beginning to pay dividends. That season was McCorkell's last, while the other pre-war stalwarts Arnold, Bailey, Herman and Heath had already left. However the highly successful new ball pairing of Shackleton – who had been selected for England in 1950 – and Cannings was already in place, the former primarily using the seam while the latter employed away swing. Neville Rogers was a very reliable opening batsman who was to score nearly 2,000 runs in 1951, and Jimmy Gray and Leo Harrison were showing promise.

HAMPSHIRE CCC 1948
Court (Secretary), Burden, Harrison, Holt, Heath, G. Dawson, Dean, Rogers, Shackleton, Gray, Taylor, H. Dawson
Arnold, C.J. Knott, E.D.R. Eager, Bailey, McCorkell. On the ground: Hill and Prouton.
[photo: courtesy of Hampshire County Cricket Club]

Hampshire v. Oxford University - 1951

The May's Bounty wicket for the match against Oxford University in June 1951 was prepared by Fred Butler, deputising during his father's illness. The cold weather affected the attendance on both the first day, a Saturday, and on the third day. The total number paying for admission over the three days was only 2,097 and gate receipts amounted to £182.

A match against Oxford University was perhaps not the most attractive fixture with which to re-assess the appeal of first-class cricket in the north of the county. Public School and University cricket was on the wane as the cradle of gifted amateur cricketers. But the 1950s was to see the final flowering of Oxbridge cricket, spawning as it did England players of the calibre of Peter May, Colin Cowdrey, David Sheppard, Trevor Bailey, Ted Dexter and Mike Smith. In the Oxford University side which played at Basingstoke the most promising player was D. B. Carr who scored 50 in the second innings. He was to play for England on MCC's season tour of India and Pakistan at the end of the season. He was later to become a notable cricket administrator.

Hampshire came into the game in good early season form and in second place in the Championship. They had just achieved an exciting win over Lancashire at Portsmouth, scoring 175 in 130 minutes, with Jimmy Gray 42 not out. They continued this form at May's Bounty and beat the University on the final day, declaring their second innings at 260-5 (the former Yorkshire player Cliff Walker, in a good partnership with Jimmy Gray, scoring a not out century) and then bowling out the University for 267 in the last innings. For Hampshire the fast medium bowler Carty, a capable deputy for Shackleton, took 7-29 in Oxford's first innings in heavy atmosphere on the Monday. These turned out to be the best figures of his career. Vic Cannings took four wickets in the second, while the 17 year-old Peter Sainsbury – in his first year as a professional - made an appearance as a substitute fielder. Leo Harrison, later to take the wicket-keeping gloves in the Championship side, was at this stage playing only as a batsman because he was, as Hampshire's fastest mover, too valuable in the field.

The 1951 season proved to be a satisfactory one for a relatively young Hampshire side, finishing in ninth place with five wins. But they had promised much more at the outset, winning three of the first four matches to head the table and remaining undefeated for the first ten matches. Ten years later some of the players in this emerging side were to be key members of the Championship-winning team of 1961 – notably Shackleton, Sainsbury, Gray and Harrison – but May's Bounty was to miss all the excitement. By the time Hampshire staged another first-class match at the ground – in 1966 – the team was once more in the process of transition, although happily several of the Championship-winning side still remained. But the game of cricket itself, resistant to change for so long, was – if not quite embracing change – having to accept it and to adapt very quickly to commercial realities in order to ensure its very survival.

Above: The Hampshire side which finished second in the Championship in 1958. *Back row left to right*: Sainsbury, Pitman, Rayment, Heath, Burden, Horton, Barnard. *Front row*: Shackleton, L. Harrison, Ingleby-Mackenzie, Marshall and Gray. Cannings is missing from this photograph.

Left: Derek Shackleton who took 163 wickets at 15 apiece during the season.

[photos: courtesy of Hampshire County Cricket Club]

THE MODERN ERA

CHAPTER SEVEN

Regular First-class Cricket at Last

Changing Times

The 1950s had seen the beginnings of changes in the game which would have been anathema to the old die-hards of the cricket establishment. In 1951 Warwickshire, already a little frowned upon at Lords as the first county to embark on commercial ventures to raise funds, then became the first to win the Championship under a professional captain. And the following year Len Hutton became the first professional to be appointed to captain the England side.

The next decade was to see traditions and institutions challenged as never before, and even cricket caught the mood. The archaic distinction between Gentlemen and Players was swept away in 1963. But it was the arrival of sponsorship which was to have the most far-reaching consequences for the game. With attendances at 3-day county matches having plummeted from 2 million in 1950 down to 700,000, cricket finally accepted the inevitable and grabbed Mammon's hand. At last it was decided to grasp the nettle of limited overs cricket with the introduction of a 65-overs competition initially sponsored by Gillette.

Hampshire, in winning the Championship in 1961 under Colin Ingleby-Mackenzie's maxim of 'wine, women and song', had done its bit to brighten the game. In its successful introduction of West Indians Roy Marshall and Danny Livingstone – following a period of residential qualification – it had also foreshadowed one of the key developments which was about to change the face of cricket in England. This was the recruitment of star players from overseas, such as Gary Sobers for Nottinghamshire, Rohan Kanhai for Warwickshire, Mike Procter for Gloucestershire and, of course, Barry Richards for Hampshire. Again it was all made possible by further sponsorship money flowing from the start of the televised John Player Sunday League in 1969.

But in 1966 Hampshire County Cricket Club was still beset with financial problems and it had mounted another membership campaign to address the problem of poor membership numbers in the north and east of the county. This was something of a chicken and egg situation, the lack of county matches in the north inevitably fuelling a lack of interest in the county game, and this in turn discouraging the club from arranging matches away from the main centres. But the club finally decided to move one of its Southampton fixtures – against neighbours Surrey in May **1966** - to May's Bounty.

By then the town of Basingstoke had fallen victim to sixties' planners and its character as a market town was to be lost for ever. Happily the area immediately around May's Bounty escaped the carnage of the new town development and the ground was preserved as a peaceful haven away from all the mayhem created in the name of progress.

A peaceful haven – May's Bounty viewed from Bounty road c. 1960

Hampshire in 1966

As for the Hampshire team, Ingleby-Mackenzie had given up the captaincy and the side which came to Basingstoke was led by Roy Marshall - the first contracted player ever to be officially appointed to captain Hampshire. Of the Championship-winning side, he still had Horton, Gray and Livingstone in the batting line-up and Shackleton and 'Butch' White to open the bowling. Bob Cottam, later capped by England on tour, was an emerging third seamer but there was a real lack of a spinner to back up Sainsbury who, unusually, had a poor season with the ball.

HAMPSHIRE CCC 1966
Wassell, Caple, Timms, White, Cottam, Horton, Keith, Castell, Barnard, Livingstone
Reed, Gray, Shackleton, Marshall, Sainsbury, L. Harrison, and Wheatley.

A More Lasting Return to May's Bounty: Hampshire v. Surrey - 1966

As Roy Marshall and Barry Reed came out to open the innings, the *Gazette* hailed the opening of "a very special match", the first at the ground in the County Championship since the war. In the event the match itself proved to be fairly ordinary, a rain-affected draw, but it was memorable in that it marked the beginning of a thirty-five year period of consecutive annual first-class fixtures at May's Bounty. This was a period that was to bring to Basingstoke many of the great players of world cricket in the second half of the twentieth century – from Sir Garfield Sobers, Barry Richards and Mike Procter to Wasim Akram, David Gower and Shane Warne.

Marshall elected to bat on a green wicket and all the top five in the order got into the thirties without really taking charge on a rain-affected first day. 'Butch' White provided some fireworks the next morning, reaching 50 in 36 minutes before Hampshire declared at 259-6. Surrey then lost three wickets – all Test players, Edrich, Stewart and Barrington – before lunch. But rain and bad light dictated proceedings from there, despite the efforts of the teams to make a match of it. Surrey declared well behind on 143-8 and Hampshire added 62 to their lead before setting a target. In the fourth innings Surrey struggled to 83-6 between the showers.

Despite the weather, which affected the gate on the second and third days, the total attendance over the three days to see the return of the county side exceeded that for any other Hampshire Championship fixture that season. The only game to attract more paying spectators was the match against the West Indian tourists at Southampton. On the first day there were 747 paying customers at May's Bounty and the takings over the whole match (reduced by the rain) reached a creditable £298 when the average elsewhere during the season was £350 at Bournemouth, £250 at Portsmouth, and only £150 at Southampton. This of course partly reflected the higher membership numbers elsewhere (thereby reducing the numbers paying on the day), particularly at Southampton, but nevertheless the club expressed itself very satisfied both with the takings and with the way in which B&NHCC had organised the event. As a result May's Bounty was rewarded in **1967** with both a Hampshire Gillette Cup fixture against the Minor Counties' champions, Lincolnshire, and a first-class match, again versus Surrey.

Hampshire v. Lincolnshire: Gillette Cup - 1967

The first taste of limited overs competition attracted 1,197 spectators who were treated to a typically scintillating pre-lunch century by Roy Marshall who was made 'Man of the Match' by the adjudicating Alec Bedser. Bedser also complimented groundsman Dick Raynbird on the quality of his wicket. Also happy with the pitch was the tear-away fast bowler 'Butch' White who took 4-8 steaming down the hill, while 'Shack' chipped in with 3-13 as Lincolnshire were all out for 141, over one hundred runs short.

Over the next thirty years or so some county medium pacers were to be flattered by their returns from the May's Bounty wicket. But the second fixture in 1967 brought together two of the very best exponents of the seam bowlers' craft in Derek Shackleton and Geoff Arnold.

Hampshire v Surrey - 1967

This game produced a closely-fought draw and another satisfactory response from the Basingstoke public, with 1,436 paying spectators (excluding members and those who bought 3-day tickets). Hampshire batted first on another lively May's Bounty track and scored 213, Geoff Arnold taking 4-14. Derek Shackleton replied in kind with 5-64 and restricted Surrey to 200. The stalwart Henry Horton scored 66 not out in the home county's second innings of 192 in what proved to be his last season. Both sides were in sight of victory when time ran out on the final day with Surrey 33 short on 189 for eight wickets.

Generally, 1967 turned out to be a disappointing season for Hampshire who finished in 12th place.

DANNY LIVINGSTONE batting at May's Bounty v. Surrey, 1967. Mickey Stewart is at slip.
[photo: courtesy of B&NHCC]

The following season saw Hampshire entertain a star-studded Warwickshire side who included the world-class West Indians Rohan Kanhai and Lance Gibbs, the former making the top score of 33 in their first innings. Hampshire won by six wickets, thanks both to a terrific century from their own world-class batsman Barry Richards, who was well supported by wicket-keeper Bryan Timms with 53, and to the bowling of Bob Cottam who took 7-61 in Warwickshire's second innings.

ROY MARSHALL and DEREK SHACKLETON lead the side out at May's Bounty in 1968 – Shack's last full season
[Photo reproduced by kind permission of 'Gazette Newspapers']

Over the next few years a new team gradually took shape as the members of the first Championship winning side retired from the game – Horton, Shackleton, White, and finally Marshall in 1972

Richard Gilliat captained the side which surprised everyone by lifting the Championship again in **1973**, based particularly on the superb batting – and catching - of Richards and Greenidge but mainly living in the memory as a team which was greater than the sum of its parts. The pace bowlers were steady – untried players like Mottram and others released by other counties, like Taylor and Herman – but were transformed into match-winners by great fielding. It was a young team, six regulars from the side of 1969 having gone. Peter Sainsbury survived from the first Championship winning side of 1961 and made a crucial contribution with both bat and ball. He headed the County's bowling averages, closely followed by another left-arm spinner, the New Zealander David O'Sullivan. They shared exactly 100 wickets. The match at May's Bounty in this Championship season was sadly washed out.

However, Sullivan had to give way to Andy Roberts as an overseas player the following season – a controversial decision at the time but, with hindsight, a very good one - and but for bad luck with the weather Hampshire would have made it two Championships in a row. But this time the Basingstoke weather smiled on the Hampshire cause and the May's Bounty match resulted in a victory by an innings over Kent.

HAMPSHIRE CCC – COUNTY CHAMPIONS 1973

Lewis, Herman, Mottram, Taylor, Greenidge, O'Sullivan
Turner, Richards, Gilliat, Sainsbury, Stephenson and Jesty.
[photo: courtesy of Hampshire County Cricket Club]

Richard Gilliat leads out the Hampshire team at May's Bounty in 1975 –
Malcolm Nash for Giamorgan was to take 14-137 to win the match, still a
ground record against Hampshire *[photo: courtesy of Gazette Newspapers]*

CHAPTER EIGHT

Loyal Support and a Winning Track

May's Bounty 'Gates'

By the late 1960s May's Bounty had at last found a more settled place in the geography of first-class cricket. And the Basingstoke public right until the present day has continued to turn out to support the County side in good numbers, often over 2,000 for Championship matches and 3,000 for Sunday League games. The ground records were set against Surrey in 1986 for a first-class match (5,000) and against Warwickshire in 1977 for a Sunday League fixture (4,300). It is not surprising that over the years a succession of beneficiaries have chosen May's Bounty as the venue for their benefit game - among them Barry Richards who was lucky enough to select the 1977 Sunday match, Richard Gilliat in 1978, Trevor Jesty in 1982, Malcolm Marshall in 1987, and most recently Adrian Aymes in 2000 who chose the ground's final National League fixture. David Turner was not so lucky in 1981 when poor weather resulted in a much-reduced crowd.

Membership numbers in the north of the county remain relatively low - 299 in Basingstoke and Aldershot combined in 1999, representing less than 7% of the total – but the paying customers at May's Bounty still significantly exceed those at Southampton. In 1999 1,668 turned out for the Championship match against Yorkshire and 1,253 for the National League game, while the average attendance at all competitions at Southampton was under 400. In gate receipts the comparison is even more stark - £12,515 taken at the Championship game at May's Bounty as against an average of £2,351 at Southampton. It must be acknowledged of course that nowadays gate receipts represent only a small proportion of the total income of county cricket clubs, but nevertheless these figures do carry some sort of message.

The May's Bounty Wicket

In 1991 Graeme Fowler, after scoring a painstaking fifty on a damp pitch, described the wicket as "constructed like shredded wheat". The groundsman, far from taking offence, merely presented him with a bowl of the cereal the next morning! Certainly the wicket has gained a reputation over the years as being 'bowler friendly' and a 'result wicket', with games typically low scoring affairs leading to definite results. But it is interesting that Mark Nicholas in his time thought it a good pitch and considered that, if anything, the advantage inclined to the batsmen - when the speed of the outfield and the shortness of the boundaries are taken into account. He should know, given his personal success there both as captain and batsman.

Of the 43 first-class matches played there, Hampshire has won 16, lost 11, and drawn 16. So 27 (63%) have led to a definite result, compared with 56% at all venues in the same years. This despite the fact that county matches at the ground have had more than their share of bad weather – ten of the sixteen draws were significantly rain-affected.

An all-too-familiar sight at May's Bounty county games
[photo: courtesy of Gazette Newspapers]

More importantly, Hampshire have found the winning habit at May's Bounty, winning 37% of games compared to their overall winning record in the same years of 26%. But it is in the modern era that Hampshire have really worked out the May's Bounty wicket. Having lost 5 consecutive matches there in the 1930s, Hampshire have lost only another 5 of the 35 played since returning to play at Basingstoke in 1966. The recent track record has been particularly impressive, the County achieving 4 straight wins in the seasons from 1995 to 1998 in matches dominated by the seamers, helped in three of the four games by winning the toss.

County batsmen have on occasions complained about uneven bounce. Colin Cowdrey and David Turner, fine players of fast bowling, were both felled by bouncers at Basingstoke deflecting attempted hook shots in the days before helmets were introduced. Turner was hospitalised for some days following his eye injury suffered against Gloucestershire in 1972, an accident which curtailed his progress at a time when he was in line for selection against Australia, having scored a magnificent hundred against the tourists a few weeks before. Cowdrey was also taken to hospital, having suffered his injury in a ferocious spell by Andy Roberts in 1974, whom Hampshire had been able to add to their Championship winning team of 1973. By then at the veteran stage, Cowdrey showed his bravery when at the end of the season he was summoned by England to Australia to do battle with Lillee and Thomson at their fastest.

Colin Cowdrey staggers on his way to hospital after being hit on the head by a ball from Andy Roberts [photo: courtesy of Gazette Newspapers]

Roberts was to prove himself the fastest bowler in the English game and was to head the bowling averages in 1974. He announced his arrival in this game, only the second Championship match of the season, with a match return of 9-39 on what the *Hampshire Handbook* called an "unpredictable" May's Bounty wicket. He was renowned for having two bouncers, a benign one which induced the hook shot and a lethal one which even the best of batsmen attempted hook only at their peril.

Another unfortunate injury occurred at the ground in the 1990 Sunday League match with Middlesex, although no blame attached to the wicket. The former England wicket-keeper Paul Downton was hit in the eye by a flying bail, as Emburey bowled Julien Wood, a freak incident which effectively ended his career.

Middlesex team-mates offer assistance to Paul Downton after his freak accident
[photo: courtesy of Gazette Newspapers]

The wicket had achieved some notoriety in the John Player League when in the mid-1970s it set the record for the two lowest scores up to that time, both by Hampshire - 43 on a drying wicket against Essex in 1972, with Boyce taking 4-6, and 76 on a pitch of uneven bounce against Warwickshire in 1975, ironically the first season that Hampshire won the trophy. The latter was just a couple of days after Malcolm Nash had taken 14 Hampshire wickets for Glamorgan in the Championship match which preceded the JPL game.

DAVID TURNER – talented and gritty left-hander who so impressed the 1972 Australians.
Suffered a serious injury at May's Bounty that year, but also has happier memories of scoring
150 not out at the ground against Middlesex in 1988.
[photo: courtesy of Hampshire County Cricket Club]

CHAPTER NINE

Great Performances

Pace Bowlers

It is no surprise perhaps that it is the bowlers who have achieved the most outstanding returns in terms of statistics. Generally May's Bounty has favoured seam bowlers rather than spinners, but to some extent this may simply reflect the fact that the faster bowlers have usually finished the job before slow bowlers were even called upon. It is interesting, however, that Jaques' match return of 14-105 in 1914 has stood the test of time. Also his first innings return of 8-67 has only very recently been overhauled by Hampshire players, first by Kevan James claiming 8-49 in 1997 against Somerset – career best figures - and then by Peter Hartley in 1999, taking 8-65 against his former county Yorkshire.

KEVAN JAMES
8-49 in 1997

PETER HARTLEY
8-65 in 1999

[photos: courtesy of Hampshire County Cricket Club]

A number of the all-time great fast bowlers – Harold Larwood, Mike Procter, John Snow, Andy Roberts, Jeff Thomson, and Malcolm Marshall - have taken wickets at cheap cost at May's Bounty, but it is the bowlers of less than express pace that have really prospered. Malcolm Nash, a left-arm medium pacer, took a career best 9-56 for Glamorgan in 1975, "swinging the ball disconcertingly" (*Daily Telegraph*). He is unfortunately best known for being on the wrong end of the world record set by Sir Garfield Sobers, six sixes in an over, but he was a very good bowler of his type especially in helpful conditions. In the second innings he secured another five wickets on a third day pitch "which behaved with strange inconsistency" to finish with 14-137, still a record haul against Hampshire at the ground. But not before Roberts had hit him for four sixes in two overs towards the end.

FEARSOME PACE – HAMPSHIRE'S WEST INDIAN FAST BOWLERS

MALCOLM MARSHALL
5-39 in 1989

ANDY ROBERTS
9 wicket match in 1974

[photos: courtesy of Hampshire County Cricket Club]

Martin, also a left-arm medium pacer back in 1938, had taken eleven wickets for Worcestershire, a feat emulated by Angus Fraser for Middlesex fifty years later. And the ten-wicket match return for Voce for Notts in 1936 was matched by another England pace bowler, John Snow, in a losing cause for Sussex in 1976.

The May's Bounty wicket was tailor-made for accurate bowlers of Derek Shackleton's type and, although near the end of his career by the time Hampshire returned to play there, he took eight wickets in the match against Surrey in 1967. In more recent times, Cardigan Connor took up this mantle and he holds the record for the most first-class career wickets at the ground (40), with a ten-wicket haul to help beat Leicestershire in 1995 his best effort, Heath Streak taking eight in the same match.

Like Kevan James, both Dick Carty with 7-29 against Oxford University in 1951 and Mike Taylor with 7-23 against his former Nottinghamshire team-mates in 1977, bagged career best figures at the ground. David Halfyard, the former Kent fast medium bowler, bowled his new county Nottingamshire to victory in 1969 on a wicket which helped the seamers throughout, taking 6-14 to dismiss Hampshire for 101 in their second innings. In the same match White in the first and Cottam in the second had each taken seven wickets for Hampshire, 7-53 and 7-32 respectively. Only world class players Barry Richards with 56 for Hampshire and Gary Sobers who scored 49 for Notts came to terms with the pitch. This was the second seven wicket haul for Cottam in two years as he had taken 7-61 – and ten wickets in the match - in the win over Warwickshire in 1968.

CARDIGAN CONNOR – most career wickets at May's Bounty
[photo: courtesy of Hampshire County Cricket Club]

In 1986 Surrey were hustled out twice in a day, the second innings only lasting 20.1 overs, remarkably after Hampshire had scored 401-5 in their innings. The Surrey batsmen Monte Lynch and Trevor Jesty – playing against his former county – shared the misfortune of each making a pair inside three hours. Of the twenty dismissals eight were for ducks, with Marshall and Tremlett doing most of the damage. With so many business guests invited to attend on the final day, the County club took the unusual step of providing £2,000 prize money for a special 40-overs challenge match which Hampshire won by ten runs. They had two injured players and so presented Basingstoke club cricketers Neil Hames and Peter Came with the chance to join the County team.

Surrey suffered again at May's Bounty three years later, losing by eight wickets when they collapsed on the final day to Bakker and Marshall who took five wickets each.

In 1988 against Middlesex 17 wickets fell on the first day to the pace bowling firstly of Fraser and Cowan and then of Ayling and Andrew, including four batsmen out first ball, but the match ended in an improbable draw after both sides recovered in their second innings. Both David Turner with 150 not out and then Mike Gatting for Middlesex with 104 batted with resolution but could not score quickly enough to force a decisive advantage.

The rain-affected match against Lancashire in 1991 was drifting inexorably towards a draw, a situation seemingly accepted by both captains, when with ten overs remaining, a great cricketer took things into his own hands. Wasim Akram, bowling fast down the hill, scythed through the lower order as Hampshire subsided from 212-6 to 221 all out to secure an improbable victory for Lancashire by 128 runs. He finished with 5-48 and won the match through sheer skill and force of personality.

Spin Bowlers

On occasion, the spinners have had their day, but only rarely. May's Bounty did not play host to Laker and Lock. Indeed, it was denied first-class cricket for much of the period of uncovered wickets when spinners were a real force in the land. Back in 1935 P.G.H. Fender had found some purchase for his medium paced leg-breaks, taking seven wickets in the match for Surrey on a pitch which was drying after exposure to the elements. Derek Underwood, the most dangerous of modern spinners in such conditions, made only a minimal impact in his one appearance first-class appearance at the ground, although he did take 3-5 for Kent in the John Player League in 1986.

However, the Middlesex and England off-spinner, Fred Titmus, usually took wickets at Basingstoke - for example 5-51 in 1973 when rain intervened with only Hampshire's first innings being completed, which unfortunately meant that the match contributed only two points to Hampshire's Championship success in 1973. In the 1968 Warwickshire match Eddie Hemmings, a future England off spinner, out-bowled his more illustrious team-mate, the great West Indian off-break bowler Lance Gibbs. He took 6-90 but seamers still had the final say as Hampshire triumphed over Warwickshire in Bob Cottam's ten wicket match. But the most outstanding performance by a slow bowler was by John Childs, the Gloucestershire left-arm spinner who in 1978 bowled his county to a victory by an innings and 164 runs by taking 8-34 in the second innings and 12-58 in the match.

The following year the May's Bounty wicket unusually helped the spinners throughout the match, Hampshire beating Derbyshire by six wickets as Cowley with his off-spin took 5-44 in the first innings and Southern, slow left-arm, 6-81 in the second. David Steele took six wickets for the visitors with his left-arm spin, but Hampshire could count themselves lucky that Geoff Miller was away on Test Match duty. This proved to be one of only three Championship victories in the 1979 season.

And of course as we have seen in 2000 Shane Warne took the art of spin bowling to a new dimension when on an unusually dry May's Bounty wicket he and Shaun Udal enjoyed a combined haul of eleven wickets in the match against Durham.

Great Batting

Harold Larwood once complained about the common acceptance in his day that a 'good' wicket really meant 'good for batsmen'. Such acceptance doubtless had its origins in the early dominance of the game by amateur batsmen. However, flat wickets are a rarity in England these days and May's Bounty is by no means alone in tending to offer something to the bowler. But once a batsman is set, he gets full value for his shots – and many of the most memorable moments at the ground have been provided by superlative batting.

ROBIN SMITH – most centuries at May's Bounty.
Here he blasts another 4 in his spectacular match-winning innings of 140 not out against Derbyshire in 1985
[photo: courtesy of Gazette Newspapers]

And it is Robin Smith who has provided many of these moments in the modern era. He has often plundered the short boundaries to stunning effect, his first four innings at May's Bounty bringing three centuries. He has since increased that number to six, including the highest score at the ground by a Hampshire player, a powerful 179 in 1996 against Northamptonshire whom were then bowled out twice in overcast conditions to lose by an innings. All told he has scored 977 runs at the ground at an average of nearly 70.

Chris Smith also did well there, averaging just below 50, and the brothers set a new record 4th wicket partnership of 161 in 130 minutes in 1985, as Hampshire won a thrilling run chase against Derbyshire with an over to spare. In a match covered in more detail in the 'Memorable Matches' section, Chris got 83 and Robin a stunning 140 not out – his most memorable moment on the ground. It proved a game which belied May's Bounty's reputation with second innings scores of 350-6 declared by Derbyshire and 380-6 by Hampshire. Indeed, Hampshire had only once in their history successfully chased a bigger fourth innings target at any venue. The captain at this time, Mark Nicholas, only scored 0 and 4 in this match, an unusual failure because he often batted superbly on the May's Bounty track. He is a very close second to Robin Smith for the number of runs he scored at the ground. His record of 973 runs at an average of 44 includes centuries against Sussex in 1982 and Yorkshire in 1984.

MARK NICHOLAS – May's Bounty a favourite ground
[photo: courtesy of Hampshire County Cricket Club]

Pride of place for the highest first-class score on the ground, however, still rests with Alan Jones who scored 204 not out for Glamorgan in 1980, the only double hundred of his career. This was an excellent batting wicket on which the runs flowed freely, with a number of other batsmen also cashing in - among them Javed Miandad with 82 and, for Hampshire, Turner 97 not out, Nicholas 89, Tremlett 84 and Cowley 80 not out.

There were other occasions when the May's Bounty pitch was not so flat but quality batting still triumphed. In 1977 David Rock as a 20 year-old scored a chanceless 106 out of a total of 226 after Clive Rice had removed both Richards and Greenidge on a wicket which was slow but inconsistent in bounce. And in the second innings of the same match Gordon Greenidge cut loose, scoring 124 including five sixes, one of which knocked out a spectator while another hit a chimney in Bounty road. Mike Taylor confirmed that this was really a bowler's strip with his career best 7-23 in 11 overs to win the match. This was Greenidge's only first-class century at May's Bounty, but he rarely failed there and he was out on three separate occasions in the nineties. One of these was a magnificent 96 out of a total of 211 against Middlesex in 1981 after Hampshire had been put in on a seaming wicket to face a pace attack comprising Wayne Daniel, Mike Selvey, and Jeff Thomson! Thomson was making one of only eight appearances which he made in his season with Middlesex.

Trevor Jesty was a class batsman who was at times indistinguishable from Barry Richards at the wicket, particularly when driving through the covers. He often batted attractively at Basingstoke, for example guiding Hampshire to victory with an undefeated 68 against Derbyshire on the spinners' wicket in 1979. His best innings at the ground – 90 on the difficult wicket in 1974 exploited to devastating effect by Roberts - provided a platform for the victory over Kent by an innings.

Robin Smith and Gordon Greenidge apart, the other great Hampshire batsmen of the

BARRY RICHARDS –
the greatest Hampshire batsman of the modern era
[photo: courtesy of Hampshire County Cricket Club]

modern era - Roy Marshall, Barry Richards, and David Gower – appeared less frequently at May's Bounty. But they all left at least one cameo to savour in the memory. Marshall was already past his best when the County returned to play at Basingstoke in 1966, but he scored a trade-mark century before lunch in the only Gillette Cup game at the ground and also hit 67 in 72 minutes in a winning run chase against Middlesex in 1970. Barry Richards made a couple of 50s, but he also took a memorable 133 off the Warwickshire attack in the 1968 Championship match – just 12 runs short of Warwickshire's first innings total - when the next highest individual score in the match was 67 from England's Dennis Amiss. Richards also scored 123 against Glamorgan in the John Player League in 1974. Likewise David Gower in 1992, against Yorkshire in the Championship, treated the Basingstoke faithful to a classic 155 made from 254 deliveries.

A batsman of comparable grace, Zaheer Abbas, scored a magnificent 132 in 1978 – half of Gloucestershire's total – made against Roberts at his quickest after his side had been put in by Richard Gilliat in damp conditions. This was the match in which Childs bowled out Hampshire twice for low scores. Another classy player, Surrey's Graham Thorpe who was to go on to play for England, took an impressive century off the Hampshire attack in 1989, but this was in a losing cause as Surrey collapsed to Marshall in the second innings.

GORDON GREENIDGE – power play at May's Bounty

Great all-rounders

There have been some excellent all round performances at May's Bounty over the years. Captain Greig's performance in the first ever county match set a high standard for others to seek to emulate. He scored 177 in two visits to the crease and took five wickets in Warwickshire's second innings. In the 1930s Norman Yardley made a big contribution to Cambridge University's triumph, with nine wickets in the match and 64 not out in the winning run chase.

Regrettably, in this modern era May's Bounty did not receive a visit from the great Somerset side of Viv Richards, Ian Botham, and Joel Garner, and so missed out on Ian Botham in his pomp. There have been compensations, however, including an appearance by arguably the greatest all-rounder of all time, Sir Garfield Sobers in 1969. His most telling contribution in that match was an innings of 49 on a very difficult wicket.

Gloucestershire were known as 'Proctershire' in the 1970s and Mike Procter did not disappoint in the 1971 match, treating the Basingstoke public to an exhibition of attacking stroke-play, as well as ferocious fast bowling. He scored a rapid 87 not out - including twenty off one over from Sainsbury – in a low scoring and rain-affected match and then typically took 4-39 in Hampshire's only innings.

Twenty years later another great cricketer, Wasim Akram of Pakistan and Lancashire, won the 1991 match with one of the more remarkable allround performances at May's Bounty. He first bludgeoned the Hampshire bowlers to all parts to score 122 and then, with the match apparently heading for a draw, took out Hampshire's lower order to finish with 5-48 and complete an unlikely win in double quick time.

John Snow was a noted England fast bowler, but although a useful batsman he was not usually thought of as an all-rounder. But in 1976 at May's Bounty he performed heroics with bat and ball for Sussex in a losing cause. He helped Sussex recover from 97-7 to 237 all out in their first knock and scored 56 out of 124 in their second, as well as taking ten wickets in the match.

CHAPTER TEN

Memorable Matches

Here the spotlight falls on some of the best matches, both from limited overs and Championship cricket, one selected from each decade in the modern era following the return of the county team to May's Bounty in 1966.

Hampshire v Leicestershire - 1969
This first Sunday League match in **1969** at Basingstoke strangely has turned out to be the closest ever of the thirty-one limited overs matches played at the ground.

Ray Illingworth had taken over the captaincy of Leicestershire in 1969 and he was to turn them into a very successful side, but he did not appear in this match. Notable members of the team at May's Bounty included the England and former Essex all-rounder Barry Knight and the Australian quick bowler 'Garth' McKenzie who had first come over to England with the Australian touring team of 1961.

This was the first season of the John Player League and one-day cricket was rather different from the game we know some 30 years on, tactics only slowly evolving to meet the demands of the limited overs format.

The Hampshire Team in 1969
Lancashire were the early pace-setters in the Sunday League, winning the trophy in 1969 and 1970, but Hampshire ran them very close in this first season, finishing only one point behind in the runners-up spot and winning twelve matches out of sixteen. An excellent fielding side and with outstanding strikers of the ball like Barry Richards and Roy Marshall, this Hampshire team was well suited to limited overs cricket. But they also finished 5th in the Championship where batting points earned through rapid scoring were now an important ingredient. They were often depleted by injuries in 1969 – Barry Richards missing the match at May's Bounty and a number of others during the season - but this provided opportunities for younger players such as Gilliat, Turner, Jesty and Lewis to come through. In June Richard Gilliat scored four hundreds, including 223 not out against Warwickshire and the fastest century of the season in 101 minutes against Essex. David Turner took an undefeated 181 off Surrey.

The Hampshire bowling attack still boasted in Shackleton, White and Cottam three seam bowlers with Test Match experience, Cottam having just toured Pakistan with MCC in 1968-69. Derek Shackleton had largely retired from Championship cricket but aged 44 he topped the county's Sunday League bowling averages with a remarkable economy rate, just over two runs per over.

Basingstoke cricket enthusiasts were used to seeing exciting limited overs matches in the town's evening Knockout Cup competition and they were not to be disappointed with their first taste of the Sunday League at county level. Indeed it could not have produced a closer finish. Then, as now, it was often the low scoring matches which provided the most excitement.

After Reed and Lewis had put on 31 for the first wicket and Roy Marshall had top-scored with 30, three wickets fell with the score at 68 and the home county struggled to build a reasonable score from that point. It was only an unbroken last wicket stand of 15, another ground record for one-day cricket which has stood the test of time, which took the Hampshire score up to 138.

John Player League
Hampshire v Leicestershire
- 1969

ROY MARSHALL

*Top-scored for Hampshire
with 30 in a low scoring game*

But Leicestershire also struggled when they batted and with ten overs left they needed 46 runs to win with three wickets in hand. Booth and McKenzie struck some useful blows, leaving just six runs to win off the final over to be bowled by White. After two singles, White caught and bowled McKenzie off the third. The fourth was a dot ball and the fifth produced a single. The crowd held its breath as, with three runs needed off the last ball, Spencer was run out before he could complete the second and Hampshire had won by just a single run.

MATCH OF THE SIXTIES
John Player League
Hampshire v. Leicestershire at May's Bounty, August 3 rd 1969

HAMPSHIRE		LEICESTERSHIRE	
B.L. Reed c Marner b. Spencer	20	M.R. Hallam st Stephenson b Shackleton	0
R.V. Lewis b Spencer	16	*P. Marner c Livingstone b Shackleton	21
*R.E. Marshall c.Tolchard b. Marner	30	+R.W. Tolchard c Stephenson b Cottam	4
D.A. Livingstone lbw b Spencer	0	C.C. Inman run out	20
K.J. Wheatley c McKenzie b Marner	2	J. Birkenshaw b Cottam	2
T.E. Jesty b Marner	12	B.R. Knight b Jesty	30
+G.R. Stephenson c Hallam b Marner	18	M. E. Norman c Stephenson b Castell	3
A.T. Castell c Marner b Knight	8	G.C. McKenzie c & b White	21
D.W. White not out	14	B.J. Booth not out	28
R.M.H. Cottam c Norman b Knight	3	C.T. Spencer run out	1
D. Shackleton not out	10	J. Cotton did not bat	
Extras	5	Extras	7
Total (40 overs, for 9 wkts)	138	**Total** (40 overs, for 9 wkts)	137

Bowling:

McKenzie	0-25	Shackleton	2-18
Cotton	0-23	White	1-40
Spencer	3-29	Cottam	2-14
Marner	4-24	Jesty	1-38
Knight	2-32	Castell	1-20

Hampshire won by one run

Hampshire v Worcestershire - 1978

The match selected from the 1970s, also from the John Player League, is chosen less for the closeness of the contest on the day than for its importance to the season's final outcome. It was a vital clash between the joint leaders at that stage in the **1978** season. It will also bring pangs of nostalgia to Hampshire supporters to remember a side which boasted world class performers such as Richards, Greenidge and Roberts, doubly so in that within a few weeks Richards and Roberts had departed, both disenchanted with the daily grind of county cricket.

Richard Gilliat had wisely chosen the fixture as his benefit match and good weather drew a large crowd for this vital match. He put Worcestershire into bat and only the New Zealand Test player Glenn Turner really managed to build an innings, so Hampshire faced a target of less than four runs an over. The tall gangly all-rounder John Rice, a very useful one-day performer, was the most successful bowler. Richards and Greenidge at their best were the most formidable opening pair in world cricket in the 1970s, but Richard's boredom with county cricket affected his performances in 1978. Nevertheless, Greenidge rose to the extra responsibility and in this match he entertained the Basingstoke crowd to a typical innings of 65 from 64 balls, including four 6's and four 4's. This side also had some good supporting batsmen in Turner, Jesty, and Gilliat – quality players in their own right - and they saw Hampshire through to an easy victory with nine overs to spare. Jesty drove the ball in majestic style, finishing on 41 not out, while Gilliat fittingly scored the winning run.

This win confirmed Hampshire's position at the top of the league and they went on to take the John Player trophy for the second time, repeating their triumph of 1975. In that campaign the match at May's Bounty had been lost, but this time the win was one of 11 victories to clinch the league. It was a close-run thing as Hampshire won only on run rate, Somerset and Leicestershire finishing with the same points tally. But it was very much deserved as it was achieved without Richards and Roberts for the second half of the season. In the run-in to the exciting climax of the season Greenidge led the way with scores of 116, 48, 2, 51 and 122.

HAMPSHIRE CCC – WINNERS OF JOHN PLAYER LEAGUE 1978
Stevenson, Pocock, Rice, Southern, Rock, Taylor, Cowley
Greenidge, Turner, Gilliat, Stephenson, and Jesty

MATCH OF THE SEVENTIES
John Player League
Hampshire v. Worcestershire at May's Bounty, July 9 1978

WORCESTERSHIRE		HAMPSHIRE	
G.M. Turner c Roberts b Rice	46	C.G. Greenidge c Humphries b Holder	65
J.A. Ormrod b Roberts	0	B.A. Richards c Neale b Gifford	13
P.A. Neale lbw b Rice	20	D.R. Turner c Humphries b Pridgeon	25
E.J.O. Hemsley lbw b Taylor	22	T.E. Jesty not out	41
B.L. D'Oliveira c Rice b Cowley	5	N.G. Cowley c Humphries b Pridgeon	1
C.N. Boyns b Cowley	1	*R. M.C. Gilliat not out	11
+D.J. Humphries st Stephenson b Rice	23	M.N.S. Taylor	
V.A. Holder b Rice	15	J.M. Rice	
*N. Gifford c Jesty b Roberts	8	+G.R. Stephenson did not bat	
A.P. Pridgeon not out	0	A.M.E. Roberts	
J. Cumbes did not bat		T.M. Tremlett	
Extras	19	Extras	6
	—		—
Total (for 9 wkts, 39 overs)	159	**Total** (for 4 wkts, 31.1 overs)	162

Bowling:

Roberts	2-21	Holder	1-36
Tremlett	0-32	Pridgeon	2-32
Taylor	1-26	Boyns	0-14
Rice	4-39	Cumbes	0-40
Jesty	0-17	Gifford	1-26
Cowley	2-5	D'Oliveira	0-8

Hampshire won by six wickets

Hampshire v. Derbyshire - 1985

The match from the 1980s has to be the Championship clash with Derbyshire in **1985**, a match which will never be forgotten by those privileged to witness the final day's play. It was also a game which showed the May's Bounty wicket in its best light, with nearly 1,200 runs being scored over the three days.

Hampshire in 1985

Seven years on and another fine side had been put in place that was to win the Sunday League the following season and was to continue to develop under the leadership of Mark Nicholas, going on – at last – to appear in one-day finals at Lords, winning the Benson and Hedges Cup in 1988 and 1992 and the Nat West Trophy in 1991. For the moment, though, the team was to come close to winning everything in 1985 and yet to finish the season without a trophy – runners-up in the Championship, semi-finalists in the Nat West (losing to Essex only on the number of wickets lost, the scores ending level), quarter-finalists in the B & H, and third in the John Player League.

Wisden commented that Hampshire "made a positive and attractive contribution to the English season … (and) … possessed perhaps the most formidable batting line-up in the county game", built primarily around Gordon Greenidge and Chris and Robin Smith, but also with Paul Terry – getting back to form after his England career was foreshortened by a broken arm suffered against the West Indian quick bowlers – and Mark Nicholas, in his first full year as captain. Sadly Trevor Jesty had departed for Surrey, aggrieved at not being offered the captaincy. As for the bowling, Malcolm Marshall was to take 95 wickets in the season and was to find good support from the emerging medium pacer Tim Tremlett who was first to 50 wickets and was to be rewarded with an England 'B' tour under the captaincy of Mark Nicholas. Also the left-arm spinner Rajesh Maru, with 73 wickets at 26 apiece, was to bring an unexpected balance to the attack.

HAMPSHIRE CCC –1985 [photo: courtesy of Hampshire County Cricket Club]

The May's Bounty fixture in 1985 was at the end of May, only the third Championship match of the season, and Hampshire came into it in excellent form, fresh from wins in the first two. Mark Nicholas won the toss and his decision to insert the opposition looked to have been rewarded when Derbyshire were 128 for 8 wickets, with all the pace bowlers getting on the act. But Moir, Newman and Warner staged something of a recovery, including a last wicket stand of 70, and were eventually all out for a more respectable 246. When they batted Hampshire also struggled and were thankful that a flamboyant innings of 64 from Malcolm Marshall raised their score to 218.

At this stage it seemed as though this would be a low-scoring game, but the match was unusual in that both sides found batting much easier as the game progressed. When Derbyshire batted again they built steadily on their lead, mainly through a painstaking 120 by Hill who batted for nearly six hours, and they were able to declare and to set Hampshire a very stiff target of 379 in 79 overs.

Kim Barnett felt confident in his declaration as it is rare to chase such a fourth innings target successfully – indeed Hampshire had only done so once before in their history, against Essex in 1983. But he had not reckoned with the short boundaries at May's Bounty nor with the power of Robin Smith who, as a 21 year-old in his first full season, had not yet fully established his reputation. Indeed, although now qualified to play for England, the selectors were to leave him out of the England 'B' squad chosen at the end of the season, though brother Chris was chosen along with Tim Tremlett.

Greenidge and Terry provided a foundation, 80 for the first wicket, but it was the 4th wicket partnership by the Smith brothers which set up a gloriously improbable victory. Together they added 161 in 130 minutes, a rate of scoring more typical of the early years of Championship cricket before defensive field placings came into vogue. Robin finished on 140 not out, his highest score up to that time, made from 165 balls. Even so the final run-in was very tense, 65 being needed from the last 7 overs with 4 wickets left, a much stiffer proposition with no fielding restrictions than the equivalent in a one-day game. Hampshire got home with an over to spare, as Smith unforgettably twice launched successive deliveries from the England spinner Geoff Miller into Castle Field.

This took Hampshire to the top of the table. Two draws followed and they were still the leaders when they met Middlesex, the eventual champions, at Bournemouth in June. Having set them a target of 265, Hampshire had Middlesex at their mercy at 82-8, only to be thwarted by an unbeaten ninth wicket partnership of 84. Their failure to push home this advantage had a crucial bearing on the final outcome and a season which had promised so much ended in disappointment. But the Basingstoke public had their memories – and there was still much more to come from Robin Smith on annual visits to May's Bounty.

MATCH OF THE EIGHTIES
County Championship
Hampshire v. Derbyshire at May's Bounty May 29, 30 and 31 1985

DERBYSHIRE First Innings

		Second innings	
*K.J. Barnett lbw b Marshall	6	c Tremlett b Marshall	17
A. Hill run out	20	c CL Smith b James	120
J.G. Wright c Parks b Connor	29	c James b Maru	44
B. Roberts lbw b Tremlett	0	lbw b Marshall	66
W.P. Fowler b James	12	c Parks b Marshall	0
G. Miller c Parks b Connor	15	c Marshall b Connor	46
R.J. Finney c Connor b Tremlett	16	not out	27
+B.J.M. Maher c Marshall b Tremlett	8	not out	18
D.G. Moir lbw b Marshall	40		
P.G. Newman not out	56	did not bat	
A.E. Warner b Connor	24		
Extras	20		12
Total (all out)	246	Total (for 6 wkts dec)	350

Bowling:

Marshall 19-5-57-2	Marshall 16-5-39-3
James 19-5-67-1	James 18-2-63-1
Connor 15.4-5-40-3	Connor 22-3-98-1
Tremlett 18-6-30-3	Tremlett 19-7-43-0
Maru 6-0-43-0	Maru 33-13-81-1
	Nicholas 4-0-23-0

HAMPSHIRE First Innings

		Second Innings	
C.G. Greenidge c Miller b Finney	17	lbw b Newman	42
V.P. Terry lbw b Warner	6	b Miller	61
*M.C. Nicholas c Moir b Finney	0	c Roberts b Newman	4
C.L. Smith b Miller	45	lbw b Moir	83
R.A. Smith c&b Moir	12	not out	140
M.D. Marshall c Roberts b Warner	64	c Roberts b Miller	8
K.D. James c&b Miller	0	c Barnett b Moir	3
R.J. Maru c Miller b Newman	32	did not bat	
T.M.Tremlett c Maher b Warner	15	not out	13
+R.J. Parks not out	10	did not bat	
C.A. Connor lbw b Newman	0		
Extras	17		26
Total (all out)	218	Total (for 6 wkts)	380

Bowling:

Warner 16-2-67-3	Warner 11-1-63-0
Finney 14-1-56-2	Finney 11-0-62-0
Newman 6.3-1-30-2	Miller 29-3-132-2
Moir 14-5-51-1	Newman 8-1-39-2
Miller 6-4-8-2	Moir 20-3-68-2

Hampshire won by six wickets

Hampshire v Nottinghamshire – 1994

The match included from the 1990s was another Championship game – this time under the four-day format - featuring an exciting run chase in which Robin Smith was once more the major figure, the two sides running each other neck and neck throughout the contest. This was almost a mirror image of the Derbyshire match in 1985, with a pattern of scores more in the classic tradition of the longer form of the game - heavy scoring on a perfect May's Bounty wicket by both teams, but this time in their first innings followed by a more even contest between bat and ball in the second, leading to the closest of finishes.

Hampshire in 1994

The season was to be a disappointing one, finishing in 14th place in the Championship and 12th in the Sunday League. Trophies had eluded the team since the Benson and Hedges triumph in 1992. Mark Nicholas was nearing the end of his period as leader, a period which had brought tremendous one-day rewards but during which Championship success remained elusive. Chris Smith had retired but Robin remained and he was to hit 5 centuries in the season. Nicholas himself was in a rich vein of form, averaging 45 with 3 centuries. Winston Benjamin had the impossible task of replacing Malcolm Marshall and was affected by injury and it was to fall to Cardigan Connor to carry the burden of the seam bowling. He rose to the task in taking 72 wickets at 24 apiece. Meanwhile Shaun Udal was very much on the up as an off spinner, winning selection for the England one-day squad and for the tour of Australia at the end of the season.

The May's Bounty fixture was the sixth Championship game of the 1994 season and Hampshire had yet to register a win. Both sides scored over 400 runs in their first innings and each had a young player scoring a maiden century, Graham Archer exactly 100 for Nottinghamshire and Sean Morris 174 with 31 fours for Hampshire, the highest first-class score for the home county at the ground up to that point. Morris and Aymes put on 160 for the 4th wicket and Hampshire declared 32 runs behind with only six wickets down. The visitors built on their lead and set Hampshire 286 to win.

Morris again batted well the second time around, this time in a partnership of 144 with Robin Smith, which the Hampshire Handbook records was "scattered with thunderous boundaries". Smith treated the crowd to another exhibition of power play but with his departure for 111, the tempo inevitably dropped. However Nicholas and Aymes stepped it up again and the home county needed eight from the final over and finally three from the last ball. In the event Maru only managed a two to level the scores and Hampshire had failed by the narrowest of margins - another memorable finish which kept the Basingstoke faithful on the edge of their seats. Although declarations had played a part, an excellent May's Bounty pitch had lasted well and provided some good cricket in a closely contested match over four days.

MATCH OF THE NINETIES
County Championship
Hampshire v. Nottinghamshire at May's Bounty, 9 10 11 13 June 1994

NOTTINGHAMSHIRE First Innings

P.R. Pollard c Maru b Udal	40		b Connor	18
*R.T. Robinson c Aymes b Benjamin	66		c Aymes b Cowans	63
G.F. Archer b Benjamin	100		lbw b Connor	57
J.C. Adams c Nicholas b Maru	31		c & b Connor	11
P. Johnson c Terry b Udal	5		c Maru b Cowans	1
+W.M. Noon lbw b Cowans	46		not out	55
K.P. Evans b Connor	50		c Aymes b Udal	13
G.W. Mike c Udal b Connor	26		c Nicholas b Udal	1
R.A. Pick not out	34		c sub b Maru	20
M.G. Fields-Buss c Terry b Maru	7		not out	2
J.A. Afford b Maru	9			
Extras	21			12
Total (all out)	**435**		**Total** (for 8 wkts dec)	**253**

Bowling:

Benjamin 33-14-59-2	Benjamin 8-3-23-0
Cowans 24-10-69-1	Cowans 23-4-66-3
Connor 29-7-95-2	Connor 19-4-51-2
Udal 45-8-145-2	Udal 19-2-61-2
Maru 25.4-6-61-3	Maru 18-9-45-1

HAMPSHIRE First Innings

V.P. Terry b Pick	41		b Pick	4
R.S.M. Morris c Adams b Mike	174		c Field-Buss b Mike	63
R.A. Smith lbw b Evans	16		b Mike	111
+M.C.J. Nicholas st Noon b Field-Buss	2		c Adams b Mike	33
+A.N. Aymes c Pick b Mike	69		c Mike b Evans	29
S.D. Udal lbw b Evans	4		c & b Adams	5
T.C. Middleton not out	32		not out	4
R.J. Maru not out	38		not out	22
W.K.M. Benjamin			c Archer b Evans	7
C.A. Connor			b Evans	0
N.G. Cowans				
Extras	27			7
Total (for 6 wkts dec)	**403**		**Total** (for 8 wkts)	**285**

Bowling:

Evans 29-11-75-2	Evans 17-1-69-3
Pick 25-5-94-1	Pick 5-0-34-1
Mike 26-7-83-2	Mike 8-1-40-3
Afford 22-5-84-0	Afford 8-0-42-0
Field-Buss 23.2-8-44-1	Field-Buss 15-1-61-0
Adams 6-2-13-0	Adams 7-0-33-1

Match Drawn

Since Mark Nicholas stepped down as captain at the end of the 1995 season Hampshire have struggled somewhat, both in Championship and one-day competitions, with a succession of young players not quite fulfilling their early promise and the overseas stars not proving quite the match-winners of the past – until the arrival of Shane Warne. Sixth place in the Championship, eighth in the Sunday League, and a Nat West semi-final appearance, all in Robin Smith's first year as captain in 1998, have proved to be the best performances.

By contrast, Hampshire had a run of four successive victories at May's Bounty up to 1998. This included the exciting win by just nine runs in 1997 when Somerset subsided to the accurate medium pace of Kevan James in the fourth innings, after Matthew Hayden – one of the more successful of the recent overseas players - had scored 63 for Hampshire on a difficult wicket to help post a target of 235 to win.

Now, in signing off in 2000 with the crushing defeat of Durham by an innings, Hampshire have made it five wins out of the last six played at Basingstoke.

POSTSCRIPT

It is a truism that you do not appreciate what you have until you lose it. And now that we seem to have lost our county match we are left to chide ourselves with the thought that perhaps we took it too much for granted, that we did not go to every match when we had the opportunity. It is amazing to think what we had so readily available to us. While football supporters in the town have to be content with the Ryman League, perhaps enlivened by the odd FA cup-tie or friendly against league opposition, May's Bounty has played host to the greatest names in world cricket, albeit for only four or five days' cricket per year.

One of the attractive features of first-class cricket has been this ready accessibility. And the retention of its county structure has meant that it has never become, like football, overly parochial or fiercely territorial. So all parts of Hampshire have been able to identify with and take pride in the county team. But something of that now stands to be lost. Hampshire cricket is not just about the city of Southampton. It is indeed ironic that, just at the time that the Hampshire club seeks to make the case for the England team to bring a One-Day International to the provinces, it is withdrawing the equivalent county-level facility from its own out-grounds. There was something engagingly feudal about the county team playing at these out-grounds, like Kings and Queens of old descending on the local lord of the manor, deigning to exercise their rights to hospitality.

If there is a message in this story of Hampshire cricket at May's Bounty it must be that the level of support, the gate receipts, and - not least - the County's playing results at the ground should not be cast aside lightly by the County Club. But there is something more - the visibility of the County team is also important at a time when the grass-roots need all the cultivation they can get. Most youngsters no longer get to play cricket at school or at the local recreation ground. They relate to role models and cricket needs to work very hard even to figure as a potential supplier of such models.

Perhaps we will simply be left to tell our disbelieving grandchildren – if they still care – that, at that little ground at the top of the town, we once saw the likes of Sir Garfield Sobers and Shane Warne play cricket.

Happily, May's Bounty is not to share the same fate as the Northlands road ground in Southampton. This is farewell to county cricket but not to the ground itself which will, it is hoped, still host events such as the Sun Life of Canada national under-15 finals. And maybe, just maybe, all is not yet lost on the county front. The consortium - with Major Ron Ferguson a prominent member -, which was formed to fight the County Club's decision and to have May's Bounty re-instated as a first-class venue, has been asked to come up with a level of guaranteed income for any future fixture. So we wait to see whether there may yet be other chapters to add to this story.

APPENDICES

June 1997 **v. Somerset**
Hampshire 204 and 189 (Hayden 63, Rose 5-53);
Somerset 159 (Holloway 73 not out, James 5-44) and 225 (Parsons 74, Holloway 59, James 8-49).
Won by 9 runs

June 1998 **v. Derbyshire**
Derbyshire 350 (Rollins 89) and 140-3 dec;
Hampshire 210-4 dec (R. A. Smith 104 not out) and 281-5 (Stephenson 75, Aymes 61 not out).
Won by five wickets

June 1999 **v. Yorkshire**
Hampshire 206 (Silverwood 5-43) and 124 (Hoggard 4-45);
Yorkshire 192 (Blakey 59, Hartley 8-65) and 141-4 (Byas 95).
Lost by six wickets

June 2000 **v. Durham**
Hampshire 340 (Brown 4-62);
Durham 83 (Warne 4-34, Mullally 3-18, Mascarenhus 3-17) and 93 (Warne 4-22, Udal 3-35).
Won by an innings and 164 runs

TOTAL FIRST-CLASS MATCHES (1906-2000) :

PLAYED 43   WON 16   DRAWN 16   LOST 11

COMPLETE LISTING OF HAMPSHIRE'S LIMITED OVERS MATCHES AT MAY'S BOUNTY

GILLETTE CUP

May 1967   **v. Lincolnshire**
Hampshire 244-8 (R. E. Marshall 102, Horton 56);
Lincolnshire 141 (White 4-8, Shackleton 3-13).
Won by 103 runs

SUNDAY LEAGUE

August 1969   **v. Leicestershire**
Hampshire 138-9 in 40 overs (R. Marshall 30, Marner 4-24);
Leicestershire 137-9 in 40 (Cottam 2-14, Shackleton 2-18).
Won by one run   HAMPSHIRE RUNNERS UP IN THE JOHN PLAYER LEAGUE

June 1972   **v. Essex**
Essex 172 in 40 (Fletcher 69, Holder 3-18, Mottram 3-42);
Hampshire 43 in 24.1 (Boyce 4-6).
Lost by 129 runs

July 1973   **v. Warwickshire**
Warwickshire 226-8 in 40 (Amiss 64, Jesty 4-44);
Hampshire 154 in 33.3 (Hemmings 4-38).
Lost by 72 runs

August 1974   **v. Glamorgan**
Hampshire 251 in 39.4 (Richards 123, Williams 5-42, Cordle 4-52);
Glamorgan 114 in 28.3 (Herman 3-14, Sainsbury 4-20).
Won by 137 runs

July 1975   **v. Warwickshire**
Hampshire 76 in 26.5 (Hemmings 4-23);
Warwickshire 78-2 in 18.3 (Jameson 40 not out).
Lost by eight wickets   HAMPSHIRE WINNERS OF JOHN PLAYER LEAGUE

May 1976   **v. Middlesex**
Hampshire 166-5 in 40 (Murtagh 40 not out);
Middlesex 148 in 37.3 (Brearley 65, Rice 3-25, Taylor 3-47).
Won by 18 runs

July 1977   **v. Warwickshire**
Hampshire 188 in 38.4 (Willis 3-18, Bourne 3-17);
Warwickshire 192-4 in 37 (Amiss 61, Kallicharran 85, Mottram 3-24).
Lost by six wickets

July 1978   **v. Worcestershire**
Worcestershire 159-9 in 39 (Turner 46, Rice 4-39);
Hampshire 162-4 in 31.1 (Greenidge 65, Jesty 41 not out).
Won by six wickets   HAMPSHIRE WINNERS OF JOHN PLAYER LEAGUE

July 1979   **v. Gloucestershire**
Hampshire 159-6 in 40 (Pocock 52 not out, Bainbridge 3-23);
Gloucestershire 139 in 38.1 (Taylor 3-18).
Won by 20 runs
June 1980   **v. Yorkshire**
Yorkshire 177-8 in 40 (Athey 57, Malone 4-39);
Hampshire 167 in 39.3 (Old 3-15, Stevenson 3-30).
Lost by 10 runs

May 1981   **v. Sussex**
Hampshire 163-6 in 34 (Jesty 62);
Sussex 164-3 in 30.3 (Gould 69 not out).
Lost by seven wickets

June 1982   **v. Kent**
Hampshire 116-4 in 22;
Kent 84-9 in 16 (Marshall 5-31).
Won on the faster scoring rate

June 1983   **v. Leicestershire**
Leicestershire 179-8 in 40 (Butcher 59);
Hampshire 180-1 in 37.2 (Terry 100 not out).
Won by nine wickets

June 1984   **v. Leicestershire**
Hampshire 188-3 in 38 (C. L. Smith 95);
Leicestershire 192-3 in 36.3 (Willey 67, Whitaker 57 not out).
Lost by seven wickets

May 1985   **v. Glamorgan**
Abandoned without a ball being bowled

June 1986   **v. Kent**
Kent 149-9 in 40 (Tremlett 3-28);
Hampshire 150-6 in 37.3 (Terry 42, Greenidge 41, Underwood 3-5).
Won by four wickets   HAMPSHIRE WINNERS OF JOHN PLAYER LEAGUE

June 1987   **v. Middlesex**
Middlesex 143 in 40 (Connor 3-39, Marshall 3-27);
Hampshire 146-3 in 38.2 (C. L. Smith 71 not out).
Won by seven wickets

June 1988   **v. Nottinghamshire**
Hampshire 206-7 in 40 (Turner 79);
Nottinghamshire 201-5 in 40 (Johnson 82).
Won by 5 runs

June 1989   **v. Warwickshire**
Warwickshire 155-9 in 39 (Kallicharan 55);
Hampshire 156-4 in 38.5 (Terry 53).
Won by six wickets

June 1990   **v. Middlesex**
Hampshire 140 in 39.5 (M. Marshall 46);
Middlesex 144-3 in 37.5 (Ramprakash 52 not out);
Lost by seven wickets

June 1991   **v. Sussex**
Sussex 172-9 in 40 (Greenfield 78 not out);
Hampshire 158 in 39.1 (Terry 42).
Lost by 14 runs

June 1992   **v. Surrey**
Hampshire 153 in 39.5 (Middleton 42, Boiling 5-24);
Surrey 157-1 in 35.3 (Bicknell 74 not out, Thorpe 53 not out).
Lost by 9 wickets

June 1993   **v. Kent**
Hampshire 198 in 50 (Wood 33);
Kent 202-3 in 34 (Ward 112, Fleming 58).
Lost by 7 wickets

June 1994   **v. Nottinghamshire**
Nottinghamshire 219 in 40 (Archer 49);
Hampshire 222-7 in 39 (Aymes 45 not out).
Won by three wickets

June 1995   **v. Leicestershire**
Leicestershire 204-8 in 40 (James 3-32, Streak 3-48);
Hampshire 123-3 in 22.5 (Nicholas 42 not out).
Won on faster run rate

June 1996   **v. Northamptonshire**
Northamptonshire 169 in 40 (Connor 5-25);
Hampshire 170-3 in 32.3 (Benjamin 104 not out).
Won by seven wickets

June 1997   **v. Somerset**
Somerset 175 in 40 (James 3-16);
Hampshire 169-9 in 40 (Keech 44).
Lost by 6 runs

June 1998   **v. Derbyshire**
Derbyshire 160-9 in 40 (Barnett 52 not out, Connor 3-27);
Hampshire 164-3 in 37.4 (R. A. Smith 88 not out).
Won by seven wickets

June 1999   **v. Yorkshire**
Yorkshire 191-9 in 45 (McGrath 75, McLean 3-27);
Hampshire 164 in 42.1 (Stephenson 42, Vaughan 4-31).
Lost by 27 runs

June 2000   **v. Durham**
Hampshire 222-5 in 45 (Stephenson 83 not out);
Durham 204 in 44 (Lewis 55 not out, Mullally 4-40).
Won by 18 runs

TOTAL SUNDAY LEAGUE MATCHES (1969; AND 1972-2000):

      PLAYED 30   **WON 16**   **LOST 13**   **NO RESULT 1**

TOTAL GILLETTE CUP MATCHES:

      PLAYED 1   **WON 1**

MAY'S BOUNTY FIRST-CLASS RECORDS

Batting

Highest team score:	for Hampshire	403-6 dec	v. Notts	1994
	v. Hampshire	461	by Camb. U.	1937
Lowest team score:	for Hampshire	61	v. Notts	1936
	v. Hampshire	64	by Surrey	1986

Highest individual score:

For Hampshire:

179	R.A. Smith	v. Northamptonshire	1996

Against Hampshire:

204*	A. Jones	for Glamorgan	1980

Highest partnerships for each wicket:

1st	152	A.W. Stovold & Sadiq Mohammed	for Gloucestershire	1978
2nd	196	J.M. Rice & M.C.J. Nicholas	v. Sussex	1982
3rd	144	R. A. Smith & J. S. Laney	v. Northamptonshire	1996
4th	161	C. L. Smith & R. A. Smith	v. Derbyshire	1985
5th	191	A. Morton & A.G. Slater	for Derbyshire	1914
6th	135	Wasim Akram & W. K. Hegg	for Lancashire	1991
7th	153	J. H. Pawle & D. G. Rought-Rought	for Cambridge University	1937
8th	129	G. S. Boyes & G. Hill	v. Worcestershire	1938
9th	77	C. Forbes & D. J. Halfyard	for Nottinghamshire	1969
10th	83	M. N. S. Taylor & J. W. Southern	v. Gloucestershire	1978

Bowling

Best innings return:	For Hampshire	8-49	K. D. James	v. Somerset	1997
	Against Hampshire	9-56	M. A. Nash	for Glamorgan	1975
Best match return:	For Hampshire	14-105	A. Jaques	v. Derbyshire	1914
	Against Hampshire	14-137	M. A. Nash	for Glamorgan	1975

MAY'S BOUNTY LIMITED-OVERS RECORDS

Batting

Highest team score: for Hampshire   251   v. Glamorgan   1974

                          v. Hampshire   228-8   by Warwickshire 1973

Lowest team score: for Hampshire   43   v. Essex   1972

                          v. Hampshire   114   by Glamorgan   1974

Highest individual score:

For Hampshire:

133   B.A. Richards   v. Glamorgan   1974

Against Hampshire:

85   A. I. Kallicheran   for Warwickshire   1977

Highest partnerships for each wicket:

1st	123	V. P. Terry & C. L. Smith	v. Leicestershire	1983
2nd	119*	D. J. Bicknell & G. P. Thorpe	for Surrey	1992
3rd	144	D. L. Amiss & A. I. Kallicharran	for Warwickshire	1977
4th	102	W. K. M. Benjamin & A. N. Aymes	v. Northamptonshire	1996
5th	69	H. Pougher & C. A. Richardson	for Lincolnshire (Gillette Cup)	1967
6th	83	N. E. J. Pocock & V. P. Terry	v. Gloucestershire	1979
7th	79	K. Greenfield & P. Moores	for Sussex	1991
8th	48	G. C. Mackenzie & B. J. Booth	for Leicestershire	1969
9th	20	T. M. Lamb & M. W. Selvey	for Middlesex	1976
10th	15*	D. W. White & D. Shackleton	v. Leicestershire	1969

Bowling

Best bowling: For Hampshire   5-25   C. A. Connor   v. Northants   1996

               Against Hampshire   6-53   M. A. Ealham   for Kent   1993

HAMPSHIRE COUNTY PLAYERS FROM BASINGSTOKE AND NORTH HAMPSHIRE

The north-east of the county has generally not been a prolific supplier of cricketers to the Hampshire team. How much this simply reflects the south-centred focus of the club - with its consequences for membership numbers - is open to conjecture. In cricket's Golden Age, however, when it was common for county cricketers still to play regularly for their club sides, there was more of a supply-line to the county from the Basingstoke & North Hants Club.

The following are cricketers, either with associations with B&NHCC or with the north and east of the county, who played for Hampshire:

The 'Golden Age'

Bacon, F. H. (a player with Hampshire 1894-1911)

A leading all-rounder for Basingstoke in the 1890s and sometime secretary and groundsman too. Played first-class cricket from 1895-1911, with one first-class century and five half-centuries for Hampshire, but his most outstanding innings was on his debut in 1894 before they achieved first-class status – 114 in 130 minutes against Warwickshire, an achievement which earned him a cheque from John May. He was appointed Secretary of Hampshire in 1903, a post he held until his death in World War 1.

Baldwin, H. (1877-1905)

A stalwart off-break bowler for Hampshire, before first-class status was achieved, then going on to take 580 first-class wickets. He was a professional and famous in his later playing days for his considerable girth. He played for B&NHCC from 1901-21. His son, H. G., born at Hartley Wintney, played for Surrey and later became a Test Match umpire.

[photo: courtesy of B&NHCC]

Belcher, G. (1905)

All-rounder for B&NHCC in the period 1904-12, he made one appearance for Hampshire, unfortunately making a pair, and also played more frequently for Berkshire. Lost his life in World War 1.

Bodington, C.H. (1901-02)

Made occasional appearances for Basingstoke from 1901 to 1913 and played in 10 games as a middle order batsman for Hampshire. Another who perished in the war.

Boxall, T. (pre-1895)

Played for B&NHCC in the 1890s, taking 7-12 on one occasion, but his appearances for Hampshire were not in first-class matches.

English, E. A. (1898-1901)

Middle order batsman who played occasionally for Basingstoke after finishing with Hampshire, but his main club was Alton. He lived to the age of 101.

Fowler, R. St. L. (1924)

A Basingstoke player with his own place in the history of the game but, due to his army career, he only made three appearances for Hampshire and twenty-eight in first-class cricket in total. His fame resulted from his performance as captain of Eton in the Eton v. Harrow match in 1910 – one of the leading sporting events in the social calendar at that time – which became known as 'Fowler's Match'. He saved an innings defeat by scoring 68 and then, with Harrow only needing 55 to win, he took eight wickets to win the match for Eton. He had played ten games for B&NHCC in 1907 and 1908. He was appointed to captain the MCC side to the West Indies in 1924-25 but the tour was postponed until the following year, by which time Fowler had died at the age of thirty-four.

Lamb, B. (1898-1901)

Played for Basingstoke as a batsman around the turn of the century and also had a spell as Secretary of the club, but his main club was that of his home town, Andover. He had four first-class games for Hampshire around the same period.

Lawson, M. B. (1901-19)

Made seven appearances for Hampshire as a fast medium bowler but his association with B&NHCC did not start until 1925. He captained Basingstoke for six years in the 1930s.

Moore, J. W. (1910-13)

A seam bowler and in club cricket a more than useful batsman who came from Hartley Wintney and played for Hampshire just before the First World War. He later became groundsman at the Thornycroft factory and played club cricket for Basingstoke and both football and cricket for Thornycroft over many years.

Rutherford, A.P (1912)

Born at Highclere, a middle order batsman and medium pace bowler who made a few appearances for Basingstoke in 1911-12 and one for Hampshire in 1912.

Rutherford, J. S. (1913)

Brother of A.P. and also born at Highclere, he was a lower order batsman and a medium pace bowler who played briefly for Basingstoke over the same period as his brother and played in eight matches for Hampshire in 1913.

Soar, T. (1895-1904)

A fast bowler – and also for some years, groundsman - for Hampshire, both pre- and post the county achieving first-class status, he also joined his fellow professional and county colleague Baldwin at the Basingstoke club.

Between the Wars

Harfield, L. (1925-31)

From Cheriton near Alresford, Lew Harfield was a forcing batsman who made 1,200 runs for Hampshire in 1929. He played in 80 matches altogether but his promising first-class career was ended prematurely by illness. He was still playing club cricket many years later, however, appearing for Portals at the age of fifty-eight in the final of the Knockout Cup at May's Bounty in 1963.

Lawson, H. M. (1935-37)

Son of M. B., Howard Lawson joined the County as an opening bowler in 1935, after developing under his father's watchful eye at the Basingstoke club. He played 45 matches for Hampshire, taking 71 wickets with swing and seam bowling, and proved particularly effective operating with the new ball.

Since the Second World War

Flint, D.P.J. (1990-95)

Darren Flint was a product of B&NHCC, a slow left-arm bowler who really spun the ball. He took a remarkable 5-32 against Gloucestershire on his debut for Hampshire in 1993, but unfortunately lost consistency, played in only 15 first-class games in total, and was released in 1995.

Harrison, B.R.S. (1957-62)

Bernard Harrison is a member of a family that has given great service to B&NHCC ever since father Reg played his first game for the club in 1936. An opening batsman, he scored heavily for the Hampshire Second X1 but never quite made a first team spot his own, deputising as required for Roy Marshall or Jimmy Gray. He was in the squad which won the Championship in 1961 and scored a century against Oxford University that season.

His brother Clive Harrison also played for Hampshire in non first-class matches and for the Second X1 when his teaching career permitted.

Jewell, G.A (1952)

Born at Axford, Guy Jewell was the mainstay of B&NHCC after the Second World War as an exceptional slow left-arm spinner but also as a very useful left-hand batsman. He played for the County 2nd X1 when on holiday from his teaching duties and he made one first-class appearance for Hampshire in 1952. He also played for Berkshire and for the Club Cricket Conference.

Timms, B.S.V. (1959-68)

Born in Ropley, Bryan Timms became the regular Hampshire wicket-keeper when Leo Harrison retired. He played twice during the Championship-winning season of 1961. In his career took 456 catches and made 70 stumpings in 232 first-class matches. He spent his last two years in the first-class game with Warwickshire (1969-71) and went on to play club cricket for Basingstoke.

Wood, J. R. (1989-93)

Julien Wood had early associations with B&NHCC, played for England schools, and was one of the MCC Young Professional staff in 1987-88. He joined the Hampshire staff in 1989 and made a very promising beginning as an attractive left-hand batsman, having a top score of 96 in his first season. That early promise was not quite fulfilled but his release at the end of the 1993 season did seem a little premature. Overall in 24 first-class games he averaged 30 with four 50s.

Udal. S.D. (1988 to date)

The most talented cricketer to emerge from the north-east corner of the county for many years, Shaun Udal the current County vice-captain was born at Cove, Farnborough, and lives in Basingstoke. He has not yet quite been able to fulfil his early potential when he looked like an emerging Test off-spinner, but he has often toiled on some unforgiving home wickets. A fine one-day player, he has represented England in ten one-day internationals.

BIBLIOGRAPHY

Altham, H.; Arlott, J.; Eager, E.D.R.,; Webber, R. (1957) *The Official History of Hampshire County Cricket Club*

Altham, H.; Swanton, E.W. (1938) *A History of English Cricket*

Arlott, J. (ed David Rayvern Allen 1989*) The Essential John Arlott*

Association of Cricket Statisticians (1988) *Cricket Grounds of Hampshire*

Bailey, P; Thorn, P.; Wynne-Thomas, P. (1984) *Who's Who of Cricketers*

Basingstoke and North Hants Cricket Club (1990) *A Celebration of 125 years at May's Bounty 1865-1990*

Basingstoke Review

Birley, D (1999) *A Social History of English Cricket*

Brooke, R. (1991) *A History of the County Cricket Championship*

Gannaway, N. (1990) *A History of Cricket in Hampshire*

Hampshire County Cricket Club Handbooks

Hampshire County Cricket Club website

Hants & Berks Gazette and *Basingstoke Gazette* – various issues

Harrison, B.R.S. and Bichard, P.M. (1966) *Basingstoke and North Hants Cricket Club, 1865-1965*

Jenkinson, N. (1993) *C.P. Mead – Hampshire's Greatest Run Maker*

Lemmon, D. (1997) *Changing Seasons – A History of Cricket in England 1945-1996*

May, J. *(1906) Cricket in North Hants*

Midwinter, E. (1992) *The Illustrated History of County Cricket*

Plumptree, G. (1990) *The Golden Age of Cricket*

Ray, F. (1904) *The Mays of Basingstoke*

Steen, R. (1993) *Guide to County Cricket*

The Daily Telegraph – various issues

The Cricketer Magazine – various issues

Williams, M. (ed 1985) *Double Century - 200 Years of Cricket in the Times*

Wilton, I. (1999) *C. B. Fry – an English Hero*

Wisden Cricketers' Almanack– various editions

Wynne-Thomas, P. *(1989) The History of Hampshire County Cricket Club*